Julian Edmund Tenison Woods

Malaysian Land and Freshwater Mollusca

Julian Edmund Tenison Woods

Malaysian Land and Freshwater Mollusca

ISBN/EAN: 9783337293185

Printed in Europe, USA, Canada, Australia, Japan

Cover: Foto ©Thomas Meinert / pixelio.de

More available books at **www.hansebooks.com**

MALAYSIAN LAND AND FRESHWATER MOLLUSCA.

By the Rev. J. E. Tenison-Woods, F.G.S., F.L.S., Hon. Mem. Roy. As. Soc. (Straits Branch).

(Plates XXVII.-XXX.).

Definition of the Region.—The species included in the following list are those indigenous to the Malay Peninsula in the states south of Keddah and the Indian Archipelago, exclusive of New Guinea. With the exception of the arbitrary line dividing the Malay Peninsula, the limits of this region form a province in natural history in the molluscan sub-kingdom. The reason for excluding New Guinea is that its fauna seems to belong more to the Pacific and Australian regions. The Philippine Islands are not included, because they form of themselves a peculiar province with very marked features, entitling them to separate consideration.

The physical geography of the Malaysian region is another reason for considering its pulmonate mollusca separately. The region consists of an immense number of islands of varying sizes, from mere barren granite rocks to continental islands like Sumatra and Borneo. All those that are of any size are densely clothed with vegetation. The climate is very hot, moist, and varies but little. Granite is the prevailing rock, with overlying palæozoic strata and a few outliers of Devonian limestone. There are also in Borneo and Sumatra rather extensive developments of carbonaceous sandstone and a few patches of tertiary limestone. The south-east portion of the region is made up exclusively of modern volcanic rocks.

It is known that climate, vegetation, and soil have all powerful influences in the development of the land mollusca, which live on decayed leaves and vegetation, flourishing best amid moisture and heat. All these conditions are found pre-eminently in the region I have specified, and perhaps in no country of the world are they more favourably united for the development of terrestrial mollusca.

Soil also has a remarkable influence. Some species prefer granite formations; but the predilection of land mollusca for limestone rocks is very striking. In the Malay Peninsula there is quite a number of small isolated limestone outliers in the form of hills and table-lands, mostly of a precipitous character. These are all distinguished by an abundance of genera and species of land-shells. The restricted habitat of some is most remarkable, and each patch of limestone seems to have its own species. It has been remarked by various naturalists how few means of dispersal the land-shells have, and thus it is that we find each island with its own fauna, no matter how small it is. Some of these species are peculiar and exceptional types. It must be admitted, however, that some types are very wide-spread, such for instance, as the forms of which *Helix citrina* L., and *Bulimus perversus* L., are the types.

It is highly probable that we have in the Malay Peninsula and its islands the remains of a very ancient continent. None of the younger formations have any place except in Sumatra and Borneo. At any rate there are no rocks which would justify the supposition that the region has been completely submerged within modern geological times. For these reasons, therefore, we have in the molluscan sub-kingdom a fauna of great antiquity. The circumstances also favour the restriction of species, because the land is so broken up into islands. Thus specific peculiarities become propagated and restricted. It may be said, in keeping with this, that though the species or varieties of the region are very numerous, yet the types are comparatively few. I take here the opportunity of noting that though I give a list of all the species enumerated by various authors known to me, I am very far from endorsing their views as to the value of the specific distinctions in any case. Probably the number of species, and even the genera, will admit of extensive reduction hereafter. In looking through a large collection with every gradation of shape and colour between one species and another, one cannot help being struck with the slender evidence on which some species rest. One is inclined to say that the species are comparatively few, but the variations are great in extent and endless in number.

Nevertheless, there are certain peculiar genera which stamp a character on the region, besides certain abnormal species. The *facies* of the region is Indian. All traces of African influences have disappeared. There is no *Achatina*, few *Pupas*, whilst *Cyclostoma* is beginning to take a subordinate place. Amongst the Cyclophoridæ we find peculiar though wide-spread types; and amongst the Helicidæ unmistakable uniformity. The individuals have all marked characters, so that a small amount of experience suffices to enable us to tell at a glance whether any individual shell is a member of the Malayan fauna.

There are in the region we are dealing with about 380 known species or varieties of land-shells divisible into the following genera:—*Streptaxis, Ennea, Vitrina, Helicarion, Nanina, Trochonanina, Hyalinia, Trochomorpha, Patula, Helix, Cochlostyla, Bulimus, Bulimina, Stenogyra, Rhodina, Glessula, Pupa, Hypselostoma, Clausilia, Cyclotus, Opisthoporus, Pterocyclos, Spiraculum, Cyclophorus, Leptopoma, Alycaus, Diplommatina, Opisthostoma, Pupina, Megalomastoma, Hybocystis, Georissa.* Of these the dominant genera are *Nanina, Helix, Cyclophorus, Bulimus,* and *Clausilia.* And this is the case in the Indian fauna. There is in fact the strongest resemblance between the relative proportion of certain genera in the two provinces; the difference being the complete disappearance from the Malayan Peninsula of *Achatina* and some other African genera. The large predominance of forms of *Helix* resembles India almost to the very number of species. The peculiar form of *Vitrina* distinguished as *Nanina*, but with slender claims to a generic position, is a feature shared by Ceylon, and to some extent by the Philippine Islands. *Nanina* is a thin, depressed, umbilicated shell, with a keel at the periphery, highly polished and with a tendency to bi-partite colouring.

Some of the peculiar genera of this region have extraordinary organs which are not seen elsewhere. Thus *Opisthoporus* is a depressed shell furnished with a little open tube behind the mouth. *Pterocyclos* has an almost similar tube formed by a notch in the peristome at its junction with the superior whorl, an arrangement which is slightly modified in an allied genus named *Spiraculum*. *Alycæus* has the last whorl swollen, constricted and strongly twisted near the mouth. All these species have peculiar opercula composed of a calcareous spiral series of concentric plates. In the family Pupininæ there are the strongest modifications of the last whorl which becomes twisted and constricted in the most erratic manner. In *Opisthostoma* it is elevated vertically in the air like an elephant's trunk. In *Hybocystis* we have a very peculiar form of land-shell, of which a full description is given at the end of the list. It is an approach to *Megalomastoma*, and may be said to be confined to Burmah and the Malay Peninsula.

As the limits of the region here dealt with are so little explored, no such things as sub-provinces can be made, unless it be in the way of considering each island a sub-province in itself. It is obvious to any one who considers the size and extent of any of the islands, that only a very small portion of them can have been well explored for their molluscan fauna. The total number of known species or varieties, amounting as it does to scarcely 400, can only be considered as an instalment of the actual census. The large island of Borneo alone might be expected to furnish such a number, when we remember how the climate, soil, and vegetation of this region favour the development of the molluscan fauna. Yet the species of Borneo can scarcely be said to be known at all.

In dealing with the genera and species of the various authors, it has already been stated that the specific or generic value in any individual case is a matter for which the authors themselves are alone responsible. Yet it must be borne in mind that the difficulty of dealing with some of the larger genera renders sub-division of some kind absolutely necessary. Thus in the immense genus

Helix it is no use to catalogue species without adopting sectional divisions, which has been done in the present list. It must be admitted that they are not easy to identify, as the features are so feeble, and there is so little to go upon. Still the sections may be of some assistance, and they are meant to have no higher value in classification.

With the genera it is different, and except in such a case as *Nanina* the divisions are well marked, and can hardly be mistaken one for another. In the smaller genera the features are very pronounced, that is genera small in point of numbers, not of size. I believe it may further be said that all the species of the genera *Trochomorpha*, *Bulimus*, *Cyclotus*, *Cyclophorus* and *Alycæus*, though perhaps not well distinguished from one another, are referable to a type which has certain well-defined geographical limits. With a little experience a species of *Cyclophorus*, for instance from the Malayan Peninsula, could be easily recognized as belonging to the region; but it would require a prolonged familiarity to distinguish between the characteristic types of the various islands, as for instance Java and Sumatra. The Bornean shells are easily recognized, though there are strong resemblances to the types of the Philippine Islands.

Amongst the shells enumerated there is no foreign element. No molluscan animals, as far as it is known, have been introduced from foreign regions, and become naturalized in the region now described; but the large introduction of European and Chinese plants will alter this state of things before long, if it has not done so already.

The following list has been taken from various sources. No special study has ever been made of the land mollusca of the Malayan Archipelago. But owing to the labours of Pfeiffer and Albers, the task of compiling this list has been very much facilitated. The whole references in the case of every species have not been given. As far as possible the references are made to three or four of the most easily accessible works, where more than one author has given a description. The work of Pfeiffer

("Monographia Heliceorum Viventium," 8 vols.), is taken as the standard, but corrected according to his most recent determinations of species before his decease as contained in "Nomenclator Heliceorum Viventium." These works with his "Monographia Pneumonopomorum Viventium," may be said to contain nearly all that has been done in this department of natural science. All that one requires in addition are the essays of Nevill, Benson, De Morgan, von Möllendorff and Hungerford, and these are principally contained in the Journal of the Royal Asiatic Society, Calcutta branch.

To facilitate reference, a catalogue of works, mentioning species quoted in the list, is given. It is not by any means intended as an exhaustive bibliography of the subject, but it is hoped that no author is omitted who has described any Malayan land shell. It may be necessary to add that I have not been able to verify the references of every species, which of course would impose a vast amount of labour, and enormously increase the time required for the preparation of the catalogue. But in a great many instances, perhaps the majority, I have consulted the original authors especially in the case of the older conchologists.

It should be mentioned that Pfeiffer's nomenclature of the families has been adopted, following also his orthography.

LAND MOLLUSCA.

Family STREPTAXIDÆ.

1. STREPTAXIS, Gray, 1837, Loudon's Magazine, n.s. I. p. 484.

Shell oval or oblong, in the young state sub-hemispherical, deeply umbilicate, irregular and oblique from the lower whorls which rapidly increase in size, receding from the axis of the upper. Near the close of the penultimate whorl the umbilicus is compressed by a return to the original axis.

Animal heliciform and like the genus *Anostoma*.

Mr. Gray established this genus for species manifesting a twist in the axis, or an irregular deviation in the disposition of the whorls, causing an unsymmetrical spiral. He divides them into many groups amongst which he includes a species of *Pupa*.

STREPTAXIS CONOIDEUS, Pfr. Mon. Hel. IV. p. 329.

Keddah State, Malay Peninsula.

S. PLUSSENSIS, De Morgan, Le Naturaliste, VII. 1885, No. 9, p. 68; von Möll. Jour. As. Soc. Beng. LV. 1886, p. 299.

Mt. Chekel, River Plus, Perak, Malay Peninsula.

S. MICHAUI (ENNEA), Crosse and Fischer, Jour. Conch. 1863, pl. 10, fig. 4, p. 357.

Pulo Condor, Gulf of Siam, between east side of Malay Peninsula and Cambodia.

S. BULBULUS (ENNEA), Morelet, Jour. Conch. 1863, pl. 10, fig. 3.

Pulo Condor.

2. ENNEA, H. and A. Adams, Gen. Rec. Moll. II. p. 171.

Shell slightly rimate, sub-cylindrical; apex obtuse, smooth, shining, hyaline; whorls flattened, the last narrow, sulcated externally in the middle, lamellate within, with a strong plait parallel to the columella; aperture sub-circular; parietal lamella extending inwards and situated close to the right margin; peristome expanded, the right margin flexuous, thickened in the middle.

ENNEA PERAKENSIS, Godwin-Austen and Nevill, Proc. Zool. Soc. 1879, p. 735, pl. 59, fig. 2; von Möll. Jour. As. Soc. Beng. l.c. p. 300.

Bukit Pondok, Gapis Pass, Perak.

(N.B.—This is one of the places referred to where Bukit Pondok is spelled Buket Pondong).

E. HUNGERFORDIANA, von Möll. Jour. As. Soc. Bengal, l.c. p. 301.

Bukit Pondok, Perak.

Family VITRINEA.

3. VITRINA, Draparnaud, 1801.   Tabl. pp. 33, 98.

Shell dextral, depressed or sub-globose, very thin, pellucid, with a very large last whorl ; no umbilicus, columella spiral ; aperture large, oblique semi-lunar, without teeth ; peristome thin, acute, not continuous.

Animal long, like a slug, and too large for the shell, tail very short ; mantle reflected over the shell-margin with posterior right lobe ; radula 100 rows of 75 : marginal teeth with a single long curved apex.

VITRINA NUCLEOLA, Stol. Jour. As. Soc. Beng. XL. pl. 4. fig. 12 ; Pfr. Nomencl. Hel. Viv. p. 28, No. 45.

Penang ; Prince of Wales Island ; Straits of Malacca.

4. HELICARION, Férussac, (1821), Tabl. Syst. des Animaux Mollusques, p. XXXI. and Voy. de Freycinet.

Shell heliciform, round oval, thin, fragile, covered with a very thin periostraca, spire short, whorls few, the last much enlarged, oblong triangular ; peristome simple, acute.

Animal like *Vitrina*, but the foot is truncate at its posterior extremity, with a caudal gland like *Arion*.

HELICARION PERMOLLIS, Stol. (as *Vitrina*) Jour. As. Soc. Beng. XLII. pl. 1, fig. 11. = *Vitrina permollis*, Pfr. Mon. Hel. VII. p. 10.

Penang.

H. BORNEENSIS (VITRINA), Pfr.   Mon. Hel. IV. p. 793 ; Nov. Conch. I. pl. 28, figs. 10-12.

Borneo.

A specimen of this shell was seen by me in the collection at Government House, Labuan, but no locality noted.

H. IDÆ (VITRINA), Pfr. Mon. Hel. IV. p. 793 ; Nov. Conch. I. pl. 28, figs. 13-15.

Celebes.

"One of Pfeiffer's figures shows a narrow orange-brown band, which is not mentioned in the description." Tryon, Man. Conch. I. p. 178. Collected in Celebes by Ida Pfeiffer, the celebrated female traveller. Proc. Zool. Soc. 1856, p. 325.

H. CELEBENSIS (VITRINA), Pfr. Proc. Zool. Soc. 1856, p. 325 ; Nov. Conch. I. p. 101, No. 172, pl. 28, figs. 16-18.

Also collected in Celebes by Madame Ida Pfeiffer ; Pfr. Mon. Hel. IV. p. 793, where the author doubts whether the species should not be referred to the genus *Helix*.

H. SUTURALIS, von Martens (HELICARION), Ostas. Zool. II. 1867, p. 183, pl. 12, fig. 2 ; pl. 5, fig. 9, a, b, c : Pfr. Mon. Hel. V. p. 17 *(Vitrina)*.

Island of Buru, Moluccas.

Sub-globose, very plainly striate at the suture ; yellowish-green, with an opaque white zone.

H. LINEOLATUS, von Mart. op. cit. p. 184, pl. 12, fig. 4 ; Pfr. Mon. Hel. V. p. 17, No. 56.

Java ; Sumatra.

H. SERICEUS, von Mart. op. cit. p. 185, pl. 12, fig. 1 ; *(Vitrina)*, Pfr. Mon. Hel. V. p. 18.

Island of Timor.

H. ALBELLUS, von Mart. op. cit. p. 186. = *Helix wonosariensis*, Mousson, in coll. = *Vitrina albella*, Pfr. Mon. Hel. V. p. 18.

Eastern Java, Wonosari. I collected a specimen on the lower slopes of Mount Tengger.

Family VITRINOIDEA.

5. NANINA, Gray, 1834 ; Pfr. Sym. I. p. 5, No. 3.

Shell heliciform, perforated, dextral or sinistral, somewhat depressed, thin, polished, particularly below ; periphery round or keeled, inner lip short, reflected, often covering the umbilicus ; outer lip simple or scarcely reflected.

Animal with two mantle-lobes covering part of front of shell ; foot long, narrow, truncate behind, with a pore like a slit, sometimes with a projection like a horn ; mantle-lobes with power to expand and retract laterally. Over 500 species ; tropical and sub-tropical Africa, Asia, and Oceanica.

N. VIRIDIS, Quoy and Gaimard, (as *Vitrina*), Voy. Astrol. II. p. 138, pl. 11, figs. 16-18 ; Lamarck, Deshayes edit. VII. p. 730, No. 7 ; H. Beck, Index II. p. 4 ; = *Helix viridis*, Pfr. Mon. Hel. I. p. 82.

Island of Celebes in the mountains near Menado, is the reference given by Q. and G. This part of Celebes, it will be remembered, is the only active volcanic portion.

N. LOWI, Issel, = *Hyalina (?) lowi*, Issel, Moll. Born. p. 38, pl. 5, figs. 16-18 ; = *Helix lowi (Hyalina?)*, Pfr. Mon. Hel. VII. p. 523.

Sarawak, Borneo.

N. TERSA, Issel, *(Macrochlamys)*, Moll. Born. p. 36, pl. 5, figs. 1-4 ; *Helix (Nanina) tersa*, Pfr. Mon. Hel. VII. p. 525 = *Nanina tersa*, Pfr. Nomencl. Hel. p. 37, No. 222a.

Borneo.

N. PERLUCIDA, Issel, *(Hyalina?)*, Moll. Born. p. 39, pl. 5, figs. 20-23 = *Helix perlucida*, Pfr. Mon. Hel. VII. p. 526.

Bintulu, Sarawak, Borneo.

N. MACDOUGALLI, Issel, Moll. Born. p. 37, pl. 5, figs. 9-12 = *Helix macdougalli*, Pfr. Mon. Hel. VII. p. 526.

Sarawak, Borneo.

N. PALMICOLA, Stol. = *Microcystis palmicola*, Stol. Jour. As. Soc. Beng. XLII. 1873, p. 18, pl. 1, fig. 10 = *Helix palmicola*, Pfr. Mon. Hel. VII. p. 100.

Penang; in cocoa-nut trees.

N. CASTANEA, Müller, = *Helix castanea*, Müll. Hist. Verm. II. p. 67, No. 262; Chemnitz, IX. pt. II. p. 135, pl. 131, figs. 1177-78, = *Nanina castanea*, Beck, Index p. 4 = *Helix castanea*, Pfr. Mon. Hel. I. p. 44.

Sumatra.

N. VITELLUS, Shuttleworth, in Cuming's list = Chemnitz, 2nd edit. Helix, No. 957, pl. 145, fig. 14 = *H. vitellus*, Pfr. Mon. Hel. III. p. 44, where it is thought possibly to be a variety of *H. citrina*, L. so commonly distributed throughout the Archipelago.

This specimen was found in Amboyna by Cuming. Celebes.

N. NEMORENSIS, Müll. Hist. Verm. II. in Index and quoted under the same name by Chemnitz, 2nd edit. Helix, No. 183, pl. 35, figs. 9-11 = Férussac, Hist. Nat. Moll. pr. 232, as *Helicella* = *Helix nemoralis*, Müll. op. cit. II. p. 62, No. 257 = *H. cretacea*, Born, Mus. p. 376, pl. 16, figs. 1-2; Chemnitz, IX. pt. II. p. 119, pl. 129, figs. 1146-47; *neuvardii*, De Haan in Menke's Synopsis = *Nanina nemorensis*, Gray, Proc. Zool. Soc. 1834, p. 59; also Beck, Index, p. 4. = *Helix nemorensis*, Pfr. Mon. Hel. I. p. 46.

Moluccas and New Ireland.

This shell was once to be found in all the old Museums in Europe.

N. BROTII, Bonnet, = *Helix brotii*, Bonnet, Rev. et Mag. Zool. XVI. 1864, p. 67, pl. 5, fig. 1; Pfr. Mon. Hel. V. p. 466. Pfr. doubts whether this specimen is really distinct from *H. nemorensis*, and whether it is really indigenous to Borneo.

N. BIMAENSIS, Mousson, Moll. Java, p. 111, pl. 21, fig. 1 = *Hemiplecta bimaënsis*, Albers, Heliceen, p. 60 = *Helix bimaënsis*, Pfr. Mon. Hel. III. p. 45 = *Nanina limaënsis*, Adams, Genera, Moll. II. p. 223.

In jungles, Bimah; Sumbawa.

N. OVIVITELLUS, Reeve, = *Helix ovivitellus*, Reeve, Conch. Icon. No. 1425, pl. 202 ; Pfr. Mon. Hel. IV. p. 22.

Amboyna.

N. HALATA, Mouss. Moll. Java, p. 112, pl. 21, fig. 2 = *Hemiplecta halata*, Albers, Heliceen, p. 60 = *Helix halata*, Pfr. in Chemn. 2nd edit. Helix, No. 929, pl. 142, figs. 9-10 ; *(Nanina)*, Pfr. Mon. Hel. III. p. 45.

Dompo, Java.

N. RAREGUTTATA, Mouss. Moll. Java p. 112, pl. 21, fig. 3 = *Helix rareguttata*, Pfr. Mon. Hel. III. p. 46.

Bimah ; Sumbawa.

N. SPARSA, Mouss. Jour. Conch. VI. 1857, p. 155, pl. 6, fig. 4 = *Helix sparsa (Nanina)*, Pfr. Mon. Hel. IV. p. 343.

Island of Bali.

N. COFFEA, Pfr. = *Helix coffea*, Pfr. Proc. Zool. Soc. 1855, p. 111 = *Nanina (Xesta) coffea*, Pfr. Versuch. p. 119 = *Helix coffea*, Pfr. Mon. Hel. IV. p. 23.

Moluccas and Island of Lombok.

N. CRESPIGNYI, Higgins, = *N. decrespignii (Xesta)*, Higgins, Proc. Zool. Soc. 1868, p. 179, pl. 14, fig. 1 = *N. decrepignyi (Xesta)*, Paetel, Catal. p. 84 = *Helix crespignyi*, Pfr. Mon. Hel. VII. p. 80.

Island of Labuan.

N. TROCHUS, Müll. = *Helix trochus*, Müll. Verm. II. p. 79, No. 275 ; Chemn. 2nd edit. Helix, No. 127, pl. 21, figs. 13-14 = *Trochus hortensis*, Chemn. IX. pt. II. p. 52, pl. 122, figs. 1055-56 = *Nanina trochus*, Beck, Index p. 4 = *N. circumdata*, von Martens = var. *Helix sulphurea*, Reeve = *H. circumpicta*, Mousson = *H. colorata*, Mousson = *Nanina (Hemiplecta) circumpicta*, Paetel, Catal. p. 84 = *Helix trochus*, Pfr. Mon. Hel. I. p. 46 ; III. p. 46 ; VII. p. 80. Also, Zeitschrift für Malak. 1851, and Chemn. Ed. Nov. Helix I. p. 160, pl. 146, figs. 3-5.

An imperforate trochiform conical shell with an obtuse vertex; white with a broad red band, which is wanting inside, about an inch high and 10 lines in diameter. This shell is said in one place to come from Macassar, and in another from the East Indies; but it is evidently a common widespread species, well-known to many earlier conchologists.

N. CIDARIS, Lamarck, = *Helix cidaris*, Lamarck, Hist. d. animaux, 43, p. 77; Deshayes' edit. p. 45 = *H. cidaris*, Delessert, Rec. de Coq. pl. 26, fig. 11; = *Nanina rapa*, Beck, Index, p. 3; = *Helix cidaris*, Pfr. Mon. Hel. I. p. 45.

Timor.

N. GLUTINOSA, Metcalfe, = *Helix glutinosa*, Metcalfe, Proc. Zool. Soc. 1851; Pfr. Mon. Hel. III. p. 54.

Borneo.

N. CITRINA, L. *Helix citrina*, L. Syst. Nat. 10th edit p. 771; 12th edit. No. 679, p. 1245.

This widely distributed and well-known shell has been described by all the ancient conchologists as far back as Lister, and, strange to say, for a species which varies a good deal, has not many synonyms. It is an umbilicate shell, orbicularly convex, with an obtuse spire; yellowish with a brown band, or with a white band or two, or a purple band joined to a white one; with varieties in which the band is red, yellow, white, blackish, and even yellowish-green. This band of colour seems to divide the shell into an upper and lower portion. There are excellent figures of the animal in the "Voyage de l'Astrolabe," pl. 11, figs. 1-4.

It is very common through the islands of the whole Archipelago and the Malay Peninsula.

N. COAGULATA, Pfr. = *Helix coagulata*, Pfr. Proc. Zool. Soc. 1856, p. 32; Mon. Hel. IV. p. 41.

Amboyna.

N. LUCTUOSA, Beck, Index, p. 3 = *Helix citrina*, var. of Müller, Chemn. and Pfr. Mon. Hel. I. p. 53.

This is a common shell like the last, and is subject to similar variations in colouring, which divide into three principal forms. Var. A: chestnut above, white below, divided at the periphery by a broad white band; umbilicus, chestnut brown. This variety is figured by Chemn. (Helix, fig. 1174). Var. B: greyish above with a brownish median (Chemn. fig. 1175). Var. C: white with a blackish-brown band. Regarded by some as quite distinct from *N. citrina*.

Moluccas, Malay Peninsula, &c.

N. FULVIZONA, Mousson, in coll.; von Martens, Ostas. Zool. II. p. 201 = *Helix fulvizona*, Pfr. Mon. Hel. V. p. 96.

This is a most variable shell with regard to its colouring. Ten different varieties are enumerated by Pfr., the type approaching somewhat to *Helix citrina*, L.

Celebes.

N. PARCIPILA, von Martens, in Monat. Akademie Berlin, 18th April, 1864, p. 264; *(Xesta)* Ostas. Zool. II. p. 192, pl. 9, fig. 1 = *Helix parcipila*, Pfr. Mon. Hel. V. p. 119.

Adenare Islands, Moluccas.

N. IGNESCENS, Pfr. = *Helix ignescens*, Pfr. Proc. Zool. Soc. 1861, p. 20, pl. 2, fig. 1 = *Nanina ignescens*, Wallace, Proc. Zool. Soc. 1865, p. 406; *(Xesta)* von Martens, Ostas. Zool. II. p. 192, pl. 9, fig. 2 = *Helix ignescens*, Pfr. Mon. Hel. V. p. 98.

Batchian Island, Moluccas.

N. MONOZONALIS, Lamarck, = *N. monozalis*, Pfr. Nomen. Hel. p. 40, No. 582 = *Helix monozonalis*, Lamarck, Hist. Nat. 1st edit. IV. p. 66, Desh. edit. p. 29 = *Helix unizonalis*, Desh. Encycl. Meth. pl. 462, fig. 6 = *Helicella unizonalis*, Fér. pr. 241, Hist. pl. 91, fig. 4 = *Nanina monozonalis*, Gray, Proc. Zool. Soc. 1834, p. 59 = *Zonites unizonalis*, Swainson, Malac. p. 331 = *Helix monozonalis*, Pfr. Mon. Hel. I. p. 72.

Swainson regards this shell as a mere variety of *N. citrina*.

Amboyna.

N. OBLIQUATA, Reeve, = *Helix obliquata*, Reeve, Conch. Icon. pl. 74, sp. 384 = *H. citrina*, var. Chemn. 2nd edit. pl. 24, figs. 1-2; = *Nanina teysmanni*, Mousson, in coll. = *N. obliquata*, von Mart. Ostas. Zool. II. p. 235 = *Helix obliquata*, Pfr. Mon. Hel. V. p. 115.

Sumatra; Borneo.?

N. NANINOIDES, Benson, = *Helix naninoides*, Benson, Ann. and Mag. Nat. Hist. IX. 1842, p. 486; Phil. Icon. II. 9, p. 2, pl. 6, fig. 3; Chemn. 2nd edit. Helix, No. 158, pl. 25, figs. 7-8; Pfr. Mon. Hel. I. p. 70.

This species varies in having distinct concentric striæ or being without them. Colour brownish or nearly white; periphery more or less distinctly keeled.

Singapore; Chusan.

N. UMBILICARIA, Leguillou, = *Helix umbilicaria*, Leguillou, Rev. Zool. 1842, p. 137; Chemn. 2nd edit. Helix, No. 63, pl. 11, figs. 14-15; Pfr. Mon. Hel. I. p. 64, V. p. 123.

Differs from the following in being a more solid shell, opaque, and smoother.

Sumatra; Banka; Java.

N. DESGRAZII, Homb. et Jacq. — *Helix desgrazii*, Homb. et Jacq. Voy. Pole Sud, Zool. V. p. 12, pl. 5, figs. 4-6; Pfr. Mon. Hel. IV. p. 42.

Sumatra.

N. JAVANICA, Lamarck, = *Helix javanica*, Lamarck, 1st edit. p. 76; 2nd edit. p. 45; Chemn. 2nd edit. Helix, No. 62, pl. 11, figs. 12-13 = *Helicella javanensis*, Fér. pr. 234; Hist. pl. 92, fig. 2 = *Nanina javanensis*, Gray, Proc. Zool. Soc. 1834, p. 59 = *N. javana*, Beck, Index, p. 4 = *Helix javanica*, Pfr. Mon. Hel. I. p. 64.

Very close to *Nanina naninoides*.

Java.

N. INDUTA, Pfr. = *Helix induta*, Pfr. Proc. Zool. Soc. 1845, p. 128 ; Mon. Hel. I. p. 79 = *Nanina induta*, Gray = *N. bataviana* [junior (?)], von Martens.

Java.

N. CONVOLUTA, Deshayes, = *Helix convoluta*, Deshayes, Fér. Hist. I. p. 401. No. 255 bis, pl. 87, fig. 2 ; Pfr. Mon. Hel. III. p. 18 = *Nanina convoluta*, Gray.

Sumatra.

N. CUTTERI, H. Adams, *Macrochlamys cutteri*, H. Adams, Proc. Zool. Soc. 1870, p. 794, pl. 48, fig. 21 = *Helix cutteri*, *(Macrochlamys)*, Pfr. Mon. Hel. VII. p. 80.

Busan, near Sarawak, Borneo.

N. AUREA, von Martens, *N. (Orobia) aurea*, v. Mart. Monatsber. Berl. Ak. Ap. 18th, 1864, p. 266 ; Ostas. Zool. II. p. 243, pl. 12, fig. 12 ; Pfr. Mon. Hel. V. p. 67.

Kepahiang, Sumatra.

N. CONSUL, Pfr. *Helix consul*, Pfr. Proc. Zool. Soc. 1854, p. 289 ; Reeve, Conch. Icon. Helix, No. 1395, pl. 198 = *Nanina (Xesta) consul*, Pfr. Vers. p 120 *Helix consul*, Pfr. Mon. Hel. IV. p. 44.

Sarawak, Borneo.

N. CINNAMOMEA, Valenc. = *Helix cinnamomea*, Valenc. Museum, Paris ; Reeve, Conch. Icon. No. 142, pl. 83 (?) = *Nanina cinnamomea*, Albers, Heliceen ; Gray, Catal. Pulmon. p. 93 ; H. and A. Adams, Gen. II. p. 22 = *Xesta cinnamomea*, Pfr. Vers. p. 120 — *Helix cinnamomea*, Pfr. Mon. Hel. I. p. 54, III. p. 62, IV. p. 42.

Penang.

N. JUCUNDA, Pfr. — *Helix jucunda*, Pfr. Proc. Zool. Soc. 1863, p. 524 ; Novit. Conch. p. 307, No. 419, pl. 74, figs. 13-14 = *Nanina jucunda (Macrochlamys)*, von Martens, Ostas. Zool. II. p. 240, pl. 12, fig. 7 = *Helix jucunda*, Pfr. Mon. Hel. V. p. 101.

Collected in the island of Labuan by Sir Hugh Low.

N. FULVO-CARNEA, von Martens, in Monatsber. Ak. Berlin, 18th April, 1864, p. 266 *(Orobia)* = *Macrochlamys fulvo-carnea*, v. Mart. Ostas. Zool. II. p. 242, pl. 12, fig. 8 = *Helix fulvo-carnea*, Pfr. Mon. Hel. V. p. 101.

Menado, Celebes.

N. MALACCANA, Pfr. = *Helix malaccana*, Pfr. Proc. Zool. Soc. 1854, p. 147 ; Reeve, Conch. Icon. Helix No. 1373, pl. 195 = *Nanina malaccana (Xesta)*, Pfr. Vers. p. 120 = *Helix malaccana*, Pfr. Mon. Hel. IV. p. 45.

Keddah, Malay Peninsula.

N. AGLAJA, Pfr. = *Helix aglaja*, Pfr. Proc. Zool. Soc. 1854, p. 289 ; Reeve, Conch. Icon. Helix No. 1396, pl. 199 *Nanina aglaja (Xesta)*, Pfr. Vers. p. 120 *Helix aglaja*, Pfr. Mon. Hel. IV. p. 46.

Sarawak, Borneo.

N. STEPHOIDES, Stol. *Macrochlamys stephoides*, Stol. Jour. As. Soc. Beng. XLII. 1873, p. 17, pl. 1, fig. 9 = *Helix stephoides (Macrochlamys)*, Pfr. Mon. Hel. VII. p. 109.

Penang Hill.

N. INFANS, Pfr. = *Helix infans*, Pfr. Proc. Zool. Soc. 1854, p. 290; Reeve, Conch. Icon. Helix No. 1417, pl. 201 ; *(Microcystis)* Pfr. Vers. p. 123 ; Mon. Hel. IV. p. 51.

Labuan and Sarawak, Borneo. It also occurs in Java, where it was named *Helix adnata* by Mousson.

N. CLAIRVILLEA, Fér. *Helix clairvillea (Helicella)*, Fér. pr. 243, Hist. pl. 91, fig. 1 *Nanina clairvillea*, Gray, Proc. Zool. Soc. 1834, p. 59 ; Beck, Index, p. 3 *Helix clairvillea*, Pfr. Mon. Hel. I. p. 43.

Amboyna.

N. WAANDERSIANA, Zollinger ; Mousson, Jour. Conch. VI. 1857, p. 154, pl. 6, fig. 1 = *Helix waandersiana (Nanina)*, Pfr. Mon. Hel. IV. p. 345.

Island of Bali.

N. BALIENSIS, Mousson, Jour. Conch. VI. 1857, p. 155. pl. 6, fig. 6 = *Helix baliensis (Nanina)*, Pfr. Mon. Hel. IV. p. 345.

Diambrana, Bali.

N. INQUINATA, v.d. Busch, *Helix inquinata*, v.d. Busch, in Phil. Icon. I. 1, p. 10, pl. 1, fig. 4; Chemn. 2nd edit. Helix No. 169, pl. 31, figs. 5-6; Pfr. Mon. Hel. I. p. 46.

Java.

N. SEMISCULPTA, von Martens, Malak. Bl. XX. 1872, p. 167; Pfr. Novit. Conch. IV. p. 123, No. 826, pl. 128, fig. 6 = *Helix semisculpta (Nanina)*, Pfr. Mon. Hel. VII. p. 87.

Celebes.

N. CINCTA, Lea, = *Helix cincta*, Lea, Obs. I. p. 168, pl. 19, fig. 68; Pfr. Mon. Hel. I. p. 54.

In the figure the columellar margin of the peristome appears thickened and dilated; = *Nanina steursii*, Shuttlew. = *N. contristata*, Mousson.

Java.

N. HUMPHREYSIANA, Lea, = *Helix humphreysiana*, Lea, Trans. Amer. Phil. Soc. VII, p. 463, pl. 12, fig. 16; Chemn. 2nd edit. Helix No. 168, pl. 31, figs. 3-4; Fér. Hist. XXXIV. pl. 2, fig. 7; von Martens, Ostas. pl. 10, fig. 4.

This shell seems somewhat widely distributed, since it is recorded from Pondicherry, Singapore, and Sumatra. It is an orbiculately conical shell, convex below, rugulosely granular, yellowish brown with a chestnut band at the periphery; spire somewhat elevated and acute, whorls six to seven, aperture oblique, simple acute, diam. maj. 53, min. 47, alt. 33 mill. Pfr. Mon. Hel. I. p. 43.

N. CORROSA, Mousson, Jour. Conch. VI. 1857, p. 156 = *Helix corrosa (Nanina)*, Pfr. Mon. Hel. IV. p. 348.

Java.

N. NOBILIS, Pfr. = *Helix nobilis*, Pfr. Proc. Zool. Soc. 1849, p. 127; Chemn. 2nd edit. Helix No. 771, pl. 125, figs. 1-2; Pfr. Mon. Hel. III. p. 69.

Borneo; var. in Philippines.

N. ARGUTA, Pfr. = *Helix arguta*, Pfr. Proc. Zool. Soc. 1856, p. 327; Pfr. Mon. Hel. IV. p. 61.

Tengger Hills, Java (written Tenga Hills in Pfr.).

N. HERKLOTSIANA, Dohrn, Malak. Bl. VI. 1859, p. 206 = *Helix herklotsiana*, Pfr. Mon. Hel. V. p. 121.

Java.

N. BATAVIANA, v. d. Busch, = *Helix bataviana*, v. d. B. in Phil. Icon. I. 1, p. 9, pl. 1, fig. 3; Chemn. 2nd edit. Helix No. 58, pl. 11, figs. 1-3; Pfr. Mon. Hel. I. p. 77.

Java.

N. SOULEYETIANA, Pfr. = *Helix souleyetiana*, Pfr. in Proc. Zool. Soc. 1851; Chemn. 2nd edit. Helix No. 950, pl. 144, figs. 16-17; Pfr. Mon. Hel. III. p. 74. (N.B.—The reference is erroneously given as 73 in Pfr. Nomen. Hel. Viv.).

Borneo.

N. DONOVANI, Pfr. = *Helix donovani*, Pfr. in Zeitschr. f. Malak. 1851, p. 26; Chemn. 2nd edit. Helix No. 967, pl. 147, figs. 8-9; Pfr. Mon. Hel. III. p. 75.

Borneo.

N. CENTRALIS, Mouss. Moll. Java, p. 17, pl. 2, fig. 1 = *N. (Hemiplecta) centralis*, Albers, Heliceen, p. 60 = *Helix centralis (Nanina)*, Pfr. Mon. Hel. III. p. 78.

Java.

N. MENADENSIS, Mousson, Jour. Conch. VI. 1857, p. 157 = *Helix menadensis*, Pfr. Mon. Hel. IV. p. 345.

Menado, Celebes.

N. RIEDELII, von Martens, Monatsber. Ak. Berlin, 18th April, 1864, p. 264 ; Ostas. Zool. II. p. 213, pl. 8, fig. 5 = *Helix riedelii*, Pfr. Mon. Hel. V. p. 131 = *H. securiformis*, Mousson, not Deshayes = *Cochlostyla riedelii*, Paetel.

Menado, Celebes.

N. CYMATIUM, Benson, = *Helix cymatium*, Benson, MS ; Pfr. Novit. Conch. I. p. 58, No. 95, pl. 17, figs. 1-2 = *Nanina cymatium (Hemiplecta)*, Pfr. Vers. p. 121 = *Helix cymatium*, Pfr. Mon. Hel. IV. p. 109.

Lancavi Island, Straits of Malacca ; Penang and Perak, Malay Peninsula.

N. CHEVALIERII, Souleyet, = *Helix chevalierii*, Soul. in Revue Zool. 1842, p. 101 ; Voy. Bonite II. p. 504, Atlas, pl. 28, figs. 24-26 ; Pfr. Mon. Hel. I. p. 120 = *Nanina chevalierii*, Albers, Heliceen.

The only locality given in the "Voyage de la Bonite" is Peninsula of Malacca.

N. SCHUMACHERIANA (HELIX), Pfr. = *Helix densa*, Adams and Reeve, Voy. of Samarang, Moll. p. 62, pl. 16, fig. 8 ; Chemn. 2nd edit. Helix No. 954, pl. 145, figs. 5-7 = *H. schumacheriana*, Pfr. Zeitschr. fr. Malak. 1850, p. 70 = *H. densa*, Pfr. Mon. Hel. III. p. 111.

Philippines ; Borneo.

N. CELEBENSIS, Pfr. = *Helix celebensis*, Pfr. Jour. Conch. X. 1862, p. 229, pl. 10, fig. 8 ; Sowerby, Jour. Conch. XV. 1867, p. 111 (Char. emend.) ; Ptr. Mon. Hel. V. p. 71.

Rhwo (Rhio ?) Island, Celebes.

N. VIRENS, von Martens, Ostas. Zool. II. p. 237 = ? *Helix tumens*, Pfr. Mon. Hel. III. p. 43 ; Reeve, Conch. Icon. fig. 477 (also cited for *H. cidaride*) = *Nanina virens*, von Martens, Ostas. Zool. II. p. 237 = *Helix virens*, Pfr. Mon. Hel. V. p. 73.

Sumatra.

N. WALLACEI, Pfr.=*Helix wallacei*, Pfr. Proc. Zool. Soc. 1858, p. 20, pl. 40, fig. 5; Chemn. pl. 164, figs. 13-15; Pfr. Mon. Hel. V. p. 96 = *Nanina wallacei*, Wallace, Proc. Zool. Soc. 1865, p. 406 = *N. (Nesta) wallacei*, von Martens, Ostas. Zool. II. p. 202, *var*. Pfr. Novit. Conch. IV. pl. 128, fig. 5.

Macassar; Celebes.

N. RAPA, (HELIX), Müller, Verm. II. p. 67, No. 261; Chemn. IX. pt. II. p. 134, pl. 131, fig. 1176; Pfr. Zeitschr. Malak. 1844, p. 178; Mon. Hel. I. p. 62 = *Helix cidaris*, Lamarck.

Amboyna.

N. BORNEENSIS, Pfr.= *Helix borneensis*, Pfr. Proc. Zool. Soc. 1849, p. 127; Reeve, Conch. Icon. pl. 196, fig. 1379; Pfr. Mon. Hel. III. p. 70.

Borneo.

N. RUGATA, von Martens, Monatsber. Ak. Berlin, 18th July, 1864, p. 528; Ostas. Zool. II. p. 229, pl. 10, fig. 3 = *Helix cidaris*, Pfr. Mon. Hel. III. p. 43 (not Lamarck); Reeve, Conch. Icon. pl. 86, sp. 464 = *Hemiplecta cidaris*, Wallace, Proc. Zool. Soc. 1865, p. 406 = *Helix clairvillea*, Reeve, Conch. Icon. Helix pl. 206. sp. 1454 (not Fér). = *Nanina cidaris*, Gray, Catal. Pulmonif. p. 114.

Celebes and Timor.

N. SUMATRENSIS, Mouss. MSS.; von Martens, Ostas. Zool. II. p. 237 = *Helix sumatrensis*, Pfr. Mon. Hel. V. p. 77.

Sumatra.

N. PEASEANA, Pfr.= *Helix peaseana*, Pfr. Proc. Zool. Soc. 1864, p. 603; Mon. Hel. V. p. 77 = *Hemiplecta peaseana*, Wallace, Proc. Zool. Soc. 1865, p. 406 = *Nanina rareguttata*, var. ? von Martens, Ostas. Zool. II. p. 206.

Timor and Buru.

N. MARTINI, Pfr.= *Helix martini*, Pfr. Proc. Zool. Soc. 1854, p. 149; Reeve, Conch. Icon. Helix No. 1356, pl. 193; Pfr. (*Caracolus*), Vers. p. 141 = *Nanina amphidroma*, von Martens,

Ostas. Zool. pl. 11, figs. 2-5 (Normal and sinistral shells) = *Nanina producta*, Mousson = *Ariophanta martini*, Semper = *Helix martini*, Pfr. Mon. Hel. IV. p. 300.

Padang, Sumatra.

N. BROOKEI, Adams and Reeve, = *Helix brookei*, Adams and Reeve, Voy. Samarang, Moll. p. 60, pl. 15, fig. 4; Chemn. 2nd edit. Helix No. 870, pl. 135, figs. 1-2; Pfr. Mon. Hel. III. p. 52 = *H. gigas*, Pfr. Zeitschr. f. Malak. 1850, p. 81.

In the mountains of Borneo.

N. HUGONIS, Pfr. = *Helix hugonis*, Pfr. Proc. Zool. Soc. 1863, p. 523; Novit. Conch. p. 304, No. 415, pl. 74, figs. 1-3; Mon. Hel. V. p. 81 = *H. sinistra*, Bonnet, Rev. Zool. 1864, p. 67, pl. 5, fig. 2 = *Nanina hugonis*, von Martens, Ostas. Zool. II. p. 225.

Collected in the island of Labuan by Sir Hugh Low.

N. REGALIS, Benson, = *Helix regalis*, Annals Mag. Nat. Hist. 1850, p. 215; Chemn. 2nd edit. Helix No. 915, pl. 141, figs. 5-6, var. 7-8 = *H. vittata*, Adams and Reeve, Voy. Samarang, Moll. p. 60, pl. 15. fig. 7.

Sarawak and Balambangan.

N. LINDSTEDTI, Pfr. = *Helix lindstedti*, Pfr. Proc. Zool. Soc. 1856, p. 387; Mon. Hel. IV. p. 31.

Malacca.

N. JANUS, Chemn. = *Helix janus*, Chemn. XI. p. 307, pl. 213. figs. 3016-17; 2nd edit. Helix No. 59, pl. 11, figs. 4-6; Pfr Proc. Zool. Soc. 1842, p. 87; Mon. Hel. I. p. 77 = *Helicella bifrons*, Fér. p. 233 = *Helix mackenziana*, Soul. Rev. Zool. 1841, p. 347 = *H. balesteriana*, Lea, Trans. Amer. Phil. Soc. VII. p. 460, pl. 12, fig. 10 = *Ariophanta janus*, Beck, Index, p. 5.

Mount Ophir, near Malacca.

N. RUMPHII, v.d. Busch, = *Helix rumphii*, v. d. Busch, Phil. Icon. I. 1, p. 9, pl. 1, fig. 2; Chemn. 2nd edit. Helix No. 60,

pl. 11, figs. 7-9 ; Pfr. Mon. Hel. I. p. 76 ; (*Nanina ?*) Symb. II. p. 20.
Island of Java.

N. CLYPEUS, Mouss. Jour. Conch. VI. 1857, p. 156 = *Helix clypeus*, Pfr. Mon. Hel. IV. p. 344.
Mount Semeru, Java.

N. NASUTA, Metcalfe, = *Helix nasuta*, Metcalfe, Proc. Zool. Soc. 1851 ; Pfr. Mon. Hel. III. p. 203.
Borneo.

N. (ARIOPHANTA) INTERRUPTA, G. Nevill, Hand-list Moll. Ind. Mus. 1878, p. 20 (n.sp. ?).
Kuala Kangsa, Perak, Malay Peninsula.

N. (RHYSOTA) sp. ? von Möllendorff, Jour. As. Soc. Bengal, LV. 1886, p. 301.
A large greenish-brown shell, with dark brown band at periphery, and broader band at umbilicus; periphery obtusely angular; spire of six whorls, coarsely sculptured. Near *N. pluto*, Pfr. from Cambodia.
Perak, Malay Peninsula.

N. (EUPLECTA) BIJUGA, Stol. Jour. As. Soc. Bengal, XLII. 1873, p. 14, pl. 1, figs. 4-7, pl. 2, figs. 16-18 (*Rotula*) = *Helix bijuga*, Pfr. Mon. Hel. VII. 1876, p. 105 = *Nanina bijuga*, G. Nevill, Handl. Moll. Ind. Mus. 1878, p. 31 ; (*Rotula*), Crosse, Jour. Conch. XXVII. 1879, p. 336.
Bukit Pondok ; Penang ; Malay Peninsula.

N. (MACROCHLAMYS) sp. 2 and a species of *Microcystis* were found at Bukit Pondok by Dr. Hungerford.

N. (MICROCYSTINA) TOWNSENDIANA, Godwin-Austen and G. Nevill, Proc. Zool. Soc. 1879, p. 736, pl. 49, fig. 1.
Bukit Pondok.

N. (KALIELLA) PERAKENSIS, G. Nevill and Godwin-Austen, Land and Freshw. Moll. Ind. I. 1882, p. 8, pl. 2, fig. 7.
Bukit Pondok, Perak.

N. (SITALA) CARINIFERA, Stol. Jour. As. Soc. Bengal, XLII. 1873, p. 16, pl. 1, fig. 8; Godwin-Austen, Land and Freshw. Moll. Ind. II. 1882, p. 35.

Penang.

6. TROCHONANINA, Mousson, 1869. Jour. Conch, 1869, p. 330.

The author states that certain Helices should be separated from the genus *Trochomorpha*, Albers (Heliceen, p. 60), under the name of *Trochonanina*, distinguished by an upper surface more or less sculptured, base polished with a callosity at the insertion of the columella.

TROCHONANINA LYCHNIA, Benson, = *Helix lychnia*, Benson, Ann. and Magaz. Nat. Hist. 2nd series, X. 1852; Pfr. Mon. Hel. III. p. 626 = *T. lycheria*, Pfr. Nomen. Hel. Viv. p. 57, No. 113.

Island of Singapore.

T. TROPIDOPHORA, Adams and Reeve, = *Helix tais*, Hombron et Jacquinot, Voy. Pole Sud, Atl. Livr. 22, pl. 7, figs. 42-45; Chemn. 2nd edit. Helix No. 782, pl. 125, figs. 32-33 = *H. thais*, Pfr. Zeitschr. f. Malak. 1849, p. 68 = *H. tropidophora*, Adams and Reeve, Voy. Samarang, Moll. p. 59, pl. 14, fig. 14 = *H. tais*, Pfr. Mon. Hel. III. p. 37.

Islands of Marquesas; Borneo.

T. CONICOIDES, Metc. = *Helix conicoides*, Metc. Proc. Zool. Soc. 1851; Chemn. 2nd edit. Helix No. 1020, pl. 153, figs. 20-21; Pfr. Mon. Hel. III. p. 37.

Borneo.

T. JENYNSI, Pfr. = *Helix jenynsi*, Pfr. Proc. Zool. Soc. 1845, p. 131; Phil. Icon. II. 11, p. 86, pl. 7, fig. 8; Pfr. Mon. Hel. I. p. 81.

Java; New Hebrides.

7. HYALINIA, Fér. 1819, Prodromus, p. 40 = *Aplostoma*, Moquin-Tandon, 1855.

Shell depressed or conical, more or less longitudinally, but not spirally striate; semi-transparent smooth and shining; umbilicus large, rarely small or none; epiphragm none, rudimentary or vitreous. Flagellum none or short, thick and steadied by a terminal muscle; mucous vesicles represente by a glandular layer. 50 sp.

Mostly Europe and North America.

HYALINIA AMBOINENSIS, von Martens, Monatsber. Berl. Ak. 18th Ap. 1864, p. 266; Ostas. Zool. II. p. 244, pl. 12, fig. 11; Pfr. Mon. Hel. V. p. 141.

Buru; Amboyua; Banda-Nera.

8. TROCHOMORPHA, Albers, 1850, Heliceen, p. 116. Section of *Helix = Geotrochus*, van Hasselt.

Shell sub-perforate, spire depressed conical; last whorl carinated at the periphery; columella very short, vertical; lip simple. 19 sp.

Mauritius; India; East Indies.

TROCHOMORPHA CONUS, Phillippi, = *Helix conus*, Philippi, coll. Pfr. Symb. I. p. 39; Phil. Icon. I. 1, p. 11, pl. 1, fig. 6; Chemn. 2nd edit. Helix No. 216, pl. 28, figs. 6-7; Pfr. Mon. Hel. I. p. 35.
Java.

T. (?) ANGULATA, Issel, Moll. Born. 1874, p. 42, pl. 5, fig. 5-8 *Helix angulata*, Pfr. Mon. Hel. VII. p. 528.
Sarawak, Borneo.

T. CEROCONUS, Pfr. = *Helix ceroconus*, Pfr. Proc. Zool. Soc. 1863, p. 523; von Martens, Ostas. Zool. II. p. 257; Pfr. Mon. Hel. V. p. 84.
Labuan.

T. LEUCOPHLOEA, von Martens, = *Helix leucophloea* (*Fruticola*) von Martens, Ostas. Zool. II. p. 269, pl. 12, fig. 11; Pfr. Mon. Hel. V. p. 85.

North Celebes.

T. CONULUS, von Martens, = *Helix conulus*, von Martens, Monatsber. Berl. Ak. 18th July, 1864, p. 523 (not *H. conula*, Pease, 1861); (*Fruticola*), Ostas. Zool. II. p. 269, pl. 13, fig. 15; Pfr. Mon. Hel. V. p. 333.

Kepahiang, Sumatra.

T. GYSSERIANA, Pfr. = *Helix gysseriana*, Pfr. Malak. Bl. XII. 1865, p. 122; Novit. Conch. Fasc. XXIII. p. 270, No. 381, pl. 67, figs. 3-5; Mon. Hel. V. p. 333.

Moluccas.

T. TERNATANA, Le Guillou, = *Helix ternatana*, Le Guill. Revue Zool. 1842, p. 138 = *H. batchianensis*, Pfr. Malak. Bl. 1860, p. 235 = *Trochomorpha batchianensis*, Wallace, Proc. Zool. Soc. 1865, p. 407 = *T. ternatana* (*Nigritella*) v. Martens, Ostas. Zool. II. p. 246, pl. 13, fig. 1 = *Helix ternatana*, Pfr. Mon. Hel. V. p. 254.

Moluccas.

T. CARINIFERA, Stol. = *Sitala carinifera*, Stol. Jour. As. Soc. Bengal, XLII. 1873, p. 16, pl. 1, fig. 8 = *Helix carinifera*, Pfr. Mon. Hel. VII. p. 103.

Penang Hill.

T. MICULA (ZONITES), Mouss. = *Zonites micula*, Mouss. Jour. Conch. VI. 1857, p. 158 = *Helix micula* (*Zonites*), Pfr. Mon. Hel. IV. p. 343.

Bali Island, Java.

T. TRICOLOR, von Martens, Malak. Bl. X. 1863, p. 134: (*Videna*), Ostas. Zool. II. p. 252, pl. 13, fig. 3 = *Helix tricolor*, Pfr. Mon. Hel. V. p. 181.

Island of Buru, Moluccas.

T. BICOLOR, von Martens, Monatsber. Berl. Ak. 18th Ap. 1864, p. 267; (*Videna*), Ostas. Zool. II. p. 252, pl. 13, fig. 2 = *Helix bicolor*, Pfr. Mon. Hel. V. p. 182.

Sumatra; Borneo.

T. ZOLLINGERI, Pfr. = *Helix zollingeri*, Pfr. Proc. Zool. Soc. 1851; Chemn. 2nd. edit. Helix No. 939, pl. 143, figs. 21-22; Pfr. Mon. Hel. III. p. 113.

Java.

T. CANTORIANA, Benson, = *Helix cantoriana*, Benson, in Ann. and Magaz. Nat. Hist. 3rd series, VII. 1861, p. 85; Pfr. Mon. Hel. V. p. 186.

Sang-sang, near Penang.

T. PLANORBIS, Less. = *Helix planorbis*, Less. Voy. de la Coq. p. 312, pl. 13, fig. 4 = *H. marginata*, Müll. (teste Beck) = *H. planorbis*, Pfr. Mon. Hel. I. p. 122.

New Guinea; Java; Borneo.

T. GORONTALENSIS, von Martens, = *T.* sp. von Martens, Malak. Bl. XX. 1873, p. 168 = *T. gorontalensis*, v. Martens in Pfr. Novit. Conch. IV. p. 124, No. 827, pl. 128, fig. 7 = *Helix gorontalensis*, Pfr. Mon. Hel. VII. p. 208.

Gorontalo, Celebes.

T. TIMORENSIS (VIDENA), von Mart. Ostas. Zool. II. p. 248. pl. 13, fig. 6 = *Helix timorensis*, Pfr. Mon. Hel. V. p. 187.

Island of Timor.

T. LARDEA, von Mart. = *Helix zollingeri*, Mouss. Coll. (not Pfr.) = *Trochomorpha lardea*, von Mart. Monatsber. Berl. Ak. 18th April, 1864, p. 267; (*Videna*), Ostas. Zool. II. p. 251, pl. 13, figs. 5-6 = *Helix lardea*, Pfr. Mon. Hel. V. p. 255.

Ceram, Moluccas.

Family HELICIDA.

9. PATULA, Held, 1837.

Isis, p. 916 ; Albers, Heliceen, p. 64 = *Eyryomphala*, Beck, 1837 = *Delomphalus*, Agassiz, 1837 = *Euryomphala*, Herrmansen, 1846 = *Discus*, H. and A. Adams (Genera II. p. 116) = *Pitys*, Harper Pease, 1871.

Shell perspectively umbilicate, discoid or turbinate, depressed, rugose or striate; whorls gradually enlarging; aperture round, toothless; lip acute; jaws smooth or slightly striate, with a more or less marked median protuberance. About 327 species, with a world-wide distribution.

PATULA QUADRISPIRA, von Mart. = *Helix quadrispira*, von Mart. Monatsber. Berl. Ak. 18th April, 1864, p. 267 = *Patula quadrispira* (*Rhytida*), von Mart. Ostas. Zool. II. p. 259, pl. 13, fig. 9 = *Helix quadrispira*, Pfr. Mon. Hel. V. p. 157.

Ceram, Moluccas.

P. OBSCURATA, Adams and Reeve, = *Helix obscurata*, Ad. and Reeve, Voy. Samarang, Moll. p. 59, pl. 14, fig. 18, (not Porro) = *H. arthurii*, Pfr. Zeitschr. f. Malak. 1854, p. 16; Chemn. 2nd edit. Helix No. 940, pl. 143, figs. 23-25 ; Pfr. Mon. Hel. III. p. 102.

Borneo.

P. LUTEA, von Mart. *Helix lutea*, von Mart. Monatsber. Berl. Ak. 18th April, 1864, p. 268 = *Patula lutea* (*Macrocycloides*), von Mart. Ostas. Zool. II. p. 260, pl. 12, fig. 16 = *Helix lutea*, Pfr. Mon. Hel. V. p. 167.

Buru, Moluccas.

10. HELIX, Linnæus.

Shell of variable form, smooth, rugose, striate, ribbed or tuberculate, sometimes pilose; orbicular-convex, planorboid, trochiform, sub-turriculated, or short buliniform (monstrosities sinistral, or with the whorls more or less uncoiled); aperture oblique, oval, or semilunar, with or without interior teeth on the margin or parietal wall; lip simple or thickened internally or reflected; umbilicus covered to widely open.

Animal capable of complete retraction within the shell; the jaw finely striate, or ribbed, sulcate, or plicate.

Radula :—central teeth tricuspid, laterals bicuspid or tricuspid, with an obsolete internal cusp; marginals usually wider than high, short, with two or three small cusps.

Distribution : — world-wide; about 3,400 species known. Pfeiffer, Albers, Beck, Swainson, Férussac, Tryon, H. and A. Adams, and others have proposed a great number of groups in which it is generally found that similar ones have a similar geographical distribution. Unfortunately there has been a lamentable want of consent amongst these and other authors as to the grouping, and there is no accepted system which is followed by the generality of conchologists; it would seem in fact as if each one had his own. In this list the system of Pfeiffer is followed, who makes 86 sections and 67 sub-sections.

Section 22, Hygromia. Sub-section 1, Fruticola.

HELIX MILIACEA, von Mart.= *H. milium*, von Mart. Monatsber. Berl. Ak. 18th July, 1864, p. 524 (not Morse, 1859) = *H. milicea*, (*Fruticola*), von Mart. Ostas. Zool. II. p. 268, pl. 12, fig. 15; Pfr. Mon. Hel. V. p. 68.

Amboyna.

H. CRYPTOPILA, Mouss.= *H. cryptopila*, Pfr. Novit. Conch. IV. p. 40, No. 711, pl. 117, figs. 10-12 = *H. helicinoides*, var. von Mart. Ostas. Zool. II. p. 270; Mouss. Jav. Moll. p. 23, pl. 2, fig. 6; Pfr. Mon. Hel. III. p, 162, V. p. 259 (not Hom. et Jacq.) = *H. cryptopila*, Pfr. Mon. Hel. VII. p. 391.

Island of Rakata ; Java.

H. EVERETTI (FRUTICOLA), H. Adams, Proc. Zool. Soc. 1873, p. 207, pl. 23, fig. 11; Pfr. Mon. Hel. VII. p. 401.

Sarawak, Borneo.

H. MENDAX, von Martens, Monatsber. Berl. Ak. 18th July, 1864, p. 524; (*Fruticola*), Ostas. Zool. II. p. 272, pl. 13, fig. 14; Pfr. Mon. Hel. V. p. 350.

Atapupu, Timor.

H. CRASSULA, Philippi, Icon. 1, 7. p. 152, pl. 5, fig. 3; Pfr. Mon. Hel. I. p. 198.

Java.

Sub-section 2, Monacha.

H. PULVISCULUM (FRUCTICOLA ?), Issel, Moll. Born. 1874, p. 43, pl. 5, figs. 24-27; Pfr. Mon. Hel. VII. p. 524.

Borneo.

Section 29, Plectotropis.

H. WINTERIANA, Pfr. Symb. II. p. 41; Philippi, Icon. 2, p. 23, pl. 2, fig. 7; Chemn. 2nd edit. Helix No. 605, pl. 95, figs. 1-2; Pfr. Mon. Hel. I. p. 202.

Java.

H. HUTTONI, Pfr. Symb. II. p. 82. = *H. orbicula*, Hutton, Jour. As. Soc. VII. p. 217. *H. huttoni*, Pfr. Mon. Hel. I. p. 202.

Himalayas; Java (?).

H. SUMATRANA, von Mart. Monatsber. Berl. Ak. 18th July, 1864, p. 523; (*Plectotropis*), Ostas. Zool. II. p. 266, pl. 13, fig. 13; Pfr. Mon. Hel. V. p. 409.

Wonosari, Java.

H. SQUAMULOSA, Mouss. MSS; (*Plectotropis*), von Mart. Ostas. Zool. II. p. 266; Pfr. Mon. Hel. V. p. 409.

Island of Madura, near Java.

Section 45, Hemicycla. Sub-section 3, Coelatura.

H. SIMPLEX, Lamarck, 42, p. 77, Desh. edit. p. 45; (*Helicogena*), Fér. pr. add. 48 bis Hist. pl. 25 B. fig. 6; Pfr. Mon. Hel. I. p. 20.

Amboyna.

Section 62, Cepolis.

H. PORCELLANA, Grateloup, Actes Soc. Linn. Bordeaux, XI. p. 410, pl. 1, figs. 5-6 ; Pfr. Mon. Hel. I. p. 346.
Lombok, near Java.

Section 65, Phania.

H. PYROSTOMA (HELICIGONA), Fér. pr. 139, Hist. pl. 15, fig. 3-4 ; Pfr. Symb. III. p. 73 ; Chemn. 2nd edit. Helix No. 401, pl. 67, figs. 4-5 = *Carocolla pyrostoma*, Gray, Ann of Phil. n.s. IX. p. 412 = *Helix pyrostoma*, Pfr. Mon. Hel. I. p. 295.
Island of Gilolo.

Section 68, Obba. Sub-section Genuinæ.

H. MAMMILLA (HELICELLA), Fér. pr. add. p. 67, Hist. pl. 25, figs. 1-2 ; Quoy and Gaim. Astrol. II. p. 93, pl. 7, figs. 3-5 (c. anim.)) ; Lamarck, Desh. edit. 163, p. 105 = *Obba mammilla*, Beck, Index, p. 30 = *Helix mammilla*, Pfr. Mon. Hel. I. p. 318.
Celebes.

H. PAPILLA, Müll. Verm. II. p. 100, No. 298 : (*Helicogena*), Fér. pr. 43, Hist. pl. 25 B. fig. 5 ; Lamarck, 79, p. 87, Desh. edit. p. 65 ; Chemn. 2nd edit. Helix No. 124, pl. 21, figs. 8-9 = *Trochus papilla*, Chemn. IX. p. 51, pl. 122, figs. 1053-54 = *Obba papilla*, Beck, Index, p. 30 = *Helix papilla*, Pfr. Mon. Hel. I. p. 318.
Celebes.

Sub-section 2, Janira.

H. CAMPANULA, Pfr. Proc. Zool. Soc. 1845, p. 65 ; var. Chemn. 2nd edit. Helix No. 694, pl. 111, figs. 13-14 ; Pfr. Mon. Hel. I. p. 321.
Indian Archipelago.

Sub-section 3, Philina.

H. LOXOTROPIS, Pfr. Zeitschr. f. Malak. 1850, p. 82 ; Chemn 2nd edit. Helix No. 871, pl. 135, figs. 3-4 ; Pfr. Mon. Hel. III. p. 226.
Island of Gilolo.

H. LORQUINI, Pfr. Malak. Bl. XII. 1865, p. 122; Novit. Conch. Fasc. 23, p. 273, No. 385, pl. 67, figs. 14-15; Mon. Hel. V. p. 345.

Moluccas.

H. QUOYI, Deshayes, = *H. undulata*, Quoy and Gaim. Astrol. II. p. 91, pl. 7, figs. 1-2 = *H. quoyi*, Desh. Lamarck, Desh. ed. 162, p. 105; Fér. Hist. pl. 73 B. fig. 4; Pfr. Mon. Hel. I. p. 373, III. p. 238; IV. p. 286; Chemn. new edit. III. p. 358; (*Ampelita*) Pfr. Vers. p. 137 = *Vallonia undulata*, Gray, Fig. Moll. An. pl. 72, fig. 3.

Celebes.

H. ATACTA, Pfr. Proc. Zool. Soc. 1861, p. 386, pl. 37, fig. 5; von Mart. Ostas. Zool. II. p. 306, pl. 16, fig. 1 = *Planispira atacta*, Wallace, Proc. Zool. Soc. 1865, p. 409 = *Helix atacta*, Pfr. Mon. Hel. V. p. 376.

Ternate; Gilolo.

H. HEROICA, Pfr. Proc. Zool. Soc. 1855, p. 114; (*Obba*), Vers. p. 137; Mon. Hel. IV. p. 291.

Celebes.

H. ATROFUSCA, Pfr. Proc. Zool. Soc. 1861, p. 22, pl. 3, fig. 3; Novit. Conch. p. 164, No. 261, pl. 45, figs. 1-3; (*Planispira*), von Mart. Ostas. Zool. II. p. 299 *Planispira atro-fusca*, Wallace, Proc. Zool. Soc. 1865, p. 409 *Helix atro-fusca*, Pfr. Mon. Hel. V. p. 382.

Island of Batchian.

H. LATIZONA, Pfr. Proc. Zool. Soc. 1863, p. 524 = *Planispira latizona*, Wallace, Proc. Zool. Soc. 1865, p. 409 = *Helix latizona*, Pfr. Mon. Hel. V. p. 394.

Ceram Island, Moluccas.

H. BICONVEXA, von Martens, Monatsber. Berl. Ak. 18th July, 1864, p. 526; Ostas. Zool. II. p. 317, pl. 16, fig. 13; Pfr. Mon. Hel. V. p. 404.

Island of Tavalli, Moluccas.

H. sororcula (Obba), von Martens, Ostas. Zool. II. p. 294, pl. 17, fig. 4; Pfr. Mon. Hel. V. p. 405.

Celebes.

H. koberltiana, Pfr. Malak. Bl. XVIII. 1871, p. 124; Novit. Conch. IV. p. 73, No. 760, pl. 121, figs. 12-13; Pfr. Mon. Hel. VII. p. 456.

Ceram.

Section 69, *Trachia*.

H. malayana, O. von Möllendorff, Jour. As. Soc. Beng. 1886, LV. p. 303.

Perak, Malay Peninsula.

H. penangensis, Stol. Jour. As. Soc. Beng. XLII. 1873, p. 24, pl. 3, fig. 1; Pfr. Mon. Hel. VII. p. 399.

Penang.

Section 72, *Planispira*.

H. exceptiuncula, Fér. pr. 176, Hist. pl. 70, fig. 1, pl. 73A, fig. 1; Pfr. Symb. III. p. 75; Mon. Hel. I. p. 311; Chemn. 2nd edit. Helix No. 453, pl. 76, figs. 1-3 = *Planispira exceptiuncula*, Beck, Index, p. 29.

Moluccas.

H. phryne, Pfr. Nomen. Hel. p. 182, No. 2530 = *H. exceptiuncula* var. Fér. Hist. pl. 73A. fig. 1 = *H. phryne*, Pfr. Proc. Zool. Soc. 1861, p. 386, pl. 37, fig. 7 *Planispira phryne*, Wallace, Proc. Zool. Soc. 1865, p. 409 = *Helix phryne*, Pfr. Mon. Hel. V. p. 311.

Ternate; Gilolo.

H. flavidula, von Mart. = *H. flaveola*, von Mart. Monatsber. Berl. Ak. 18th July, 1864, p. 525 (not Kryn, 1837) *H. flavidula*, von Mart. Günth. Zool. Jahresber. 1864; (*Planispira*) Ostas. Zool. II. p. 302, pl. 14, fig. 4; Pfr. Mon. Hel. V. p. 378.

Maros, Celebes.

H. quadrifasciata, Le Guill. Revue Zoologique, 1842, p. 141; Pfr. Mon. Hel. I. p. 381.

Ternate; Halmahera.

H. ENDOPTYCHA, von Mart. Monatsber. Berl. Ak. 18th Ap. 1864, p. 268 ; (*Planispira*), Ostas. Zool. II. p. 301, pl. 14, fig. 2 ; Pfr. Mon. Hel. V. p. 383.

Ternate ; Batjan (? Batchian).

H. ZONALIS (HELICELLA), Fér. pr. 175, Hist. pl. 70, fig. 3 ; Pfr. Symb. II. p. 42 ; Mon. Hel. I. p. 380 ; Chemn. 2nd edit. Helix No. 24, p. 50, pl. 6, figs. 14-15 = *H. zonaria*, Chemn. IX. Pt. 2, p. 140, pl. 132, fig. 1188 = *Planispira zonalis*, Beck, Index, p. 30.

Gilolo.

H. (DORCASIA) COMPTA, H. Adams, Proc. Zool. Soc. 1865, p. 414, pl. 21, fig. 8 ; Pfr. Mon. Hel. V. p. 380.

Batchian.

H. KURRI, Pfr. Proc. Zool. Soc. 1847 ; Mon. Hel. I. p. 386.

Ceram.

H. ZONARIA, L. Syst. Nat. 12th edit. p. 1245, No. 681 ; (*Helicella*), Fér. pr. 177, Hist. pl. 71, figs. 6-10, pl. 73, figs. 3-10 ; Lamarck, 37, p. 75, Desh. edit. p. 44 ; Fér. Voy. de Freycin. Zool. p. 469, pl. 67, figs. 14-15 ; Quoy and Gaim. Astrol. II. p. 104, pl. 8, fig. 14 ; Chemn. 2nd edit. Helix No. 569, pl. 14, figs. 11-12, pl. 90, figs. 13-18 = *Planispira zonaria*, Beck, Index, p. 30 = *Pusiodon zonaria*, Swains. Malac. p. 330 : Knorr, Vergnüg. V. p. 33, pl. 21, fig. 41 ; Pfr. Mon. Hel. I. p. 386.

Amboyna ; Ceram ; Buru.

H. FASCIOLATA, Lesson (?), Voy. Coq. Zool. II. 1, p. 311 (?) ; (*Planispira*), von Mart. Ostas. Zool. II. p. 314 ; Pfr. Mon. Hel V. p. 505.

Moluccas.

H. COLLIS, Mouss. in coll. Pfr. Novit. Conch. IV. Fasc. 39, p. 36, No. 708, pl. 117, figs. 1-3 = *H. zonaria*, var. von Mart. Ostas. Zool. Moll. p. 312 = *H. collis*, Pfr. Mon. Hel. VII. p. 444

Amboyna.

H. COLUBER, Beck,=*Planispira coluber*, Beck, Index, p. 30 = *Helix coluber*, Chemn. 2nd edit. Helix No. 23, p. 49, pl. 6, figs. 8-9 = *H. zonaria*, Chemn. IX. Pt. 2, p. 140, pl. 132, fig. 1189 ; var. Fér. Hist. pl. 73, figs. 1-2 ; Knorr, Vergnüg. V. p. 33, pl. 21, fig. 3 = *H. coluber*, Pfr. Mon. Hel. I. p. 386.

Gilolo.

H. MERSISPIRA, von Mart. Monatsber. Berl. Ak. 18th July, 1864, p. 525 ; (*Planispira*), Ostas. Zool. II. p. 303, pl. 14, fig. 8 ; Pfr. Mon. Hel. V. p. 388.

Island of Moti, Moluccas.

H. AURITA, von Mart. Monatsber. Berl. Ak. 18th April, 1864, p. 269 ; (*Chloritis*), Ostas. Zool. II. p. 316, pl. 16, fig. 12 ; Pfr. Mon. Hel. V. p. 389.

Moti Island, Moluccas.

H. GUTTATA, Le Guill. Revue Zool. 1842, p. 141 ; Pfr. Mon. Hel. I. p. 388.

Ceram.

H. ZEBRA, Pfr. Zeitschr. f. Malak. 1850, p. 83 ; Chemn. 2nd edit. Helix No. 875, pl. 135, figs. 16-18 ; Reeve, Conch. Icon. No. 499, pl. 92 = *H. zonaria*, var. Fér. Hist. pl. 73, fig. 5 ? = *H. zebra*, Pfr. Mon. Hel. III. p. 246.

Ceram ; Goram.

H. EXPANSA, Pfr. Proc. Zool. Soc. 1861, p. 22 ; Novit. Conch. p. 165, No. 262, pl. 45, figs. 4-6 ; (*Chloritis*), von Mart. Ostas. Zool. II. p. 286, pl. 14, fig. 3 = *H. anozona*, von Mart. Monatsber. Berl. Ak. 18th Ap. 1864, p. 269 = *Planispira expansa*, Wallace, Proc. Zool. Soc. 1865, p. 409 = *Helix expansa*, Pfr. Mon. Hel. V. p. 391.

Batchian.

H. MARGARITUS, Pfr. Zeitschr. f. Malak. 1850, p. 83 ; Chemn. 2nd edit. Helix No. 876, pl. 135, figs. 19-21 ; Pfr. Mon. Hel III. p. 246.

Moluccas.

H. EMBRECHTIANA, Mouss in coll.; Pfr. Novit. Conch. IV. p. 39, No. 710, pl. 117, figs. 7-9; Mon. Hel. VII. p. 446 (erroneously marked p. 746 in Nomen. Hel.)

Moluccas.

Section 73, *Chloritis*.

H. ZODIACA, Fér. (HELICELLA) pr 184, Hist. pl. 75, fig. 2; Pfr. Sym. III. p. 78 = *H. zodiacus*, Wood, Suppl. pl. 7, fig. 52 = *Ampelita zodiaca*, Beck, Index, p. 30 = *Helix zodiaca*, Pfr. Mon. Hel. I. p. 373.

Celebes.

H. TUBA, Albers, Malak. Bl. 1854, p. 214; Pfr. Novit. Conch. I. p. 25, No. 41, pl. 7, figs. 1-3; (*Ampelita*), Pfr. Vers. p. 137; Mon. Hel. IV. p. 288.

Celebes.

H. BULBULUS, Mouss. = *H. bulbus*, Mouss. Jav. Moll. p. 113, pl. 21, fig. 5 = *H. bulbulus*, Mouss. MSS.; Pfr. Mon. Hel. III. p. 271.

Maros, Celebes.

H. UNGULINA, L. Syst. ed. 10, p. 772, ed. 12, p. 1245; Pfr. Mon. Hel. I p. 383.

Ceram.

H. UNGUICULASTRA, von Martens, Monatsber. Berl. Ak. 18th July, 1864, p. 524; *(Chloritis)*, Ostas. Zool. II. p. 281, pl. 14, fig. 1; var. *pilosa*, von Mart. Ostas. Zool. II. p. 282; Pfr. Mon. Hel. V. p. 386.

Amboyna and Buru.

H. CERAMENSIS, Pfr. Proc. Zool. Soc. 1861, p. 192; *(Chloritis)*, von Mart. Ostas. Zool. II. p. 283 *Semicornu ceramense*, Wallace, Proc. Zool. Soc. 1865, p. 410 = *Helix ceramensis*, Pfr. Mon. Hel. V. p. 386.

Ceram.

H. UNGUICULA, (HELICELLA), Fér. pr. 191, Hist. pl. 76, figs. 3-4; Lamarck, Desh. edit. 151, p. 99; Desh. in Fér. Hist. p. 12; Chemn. 2nd edit. Helix No. 38, pl. 8, figs. 10-11 = *H. ungulina*, Chemn. IX. P. 2, p. 81, pl. 125, figs. 1098-99 = *Chloritis unguicula*, Beck, Index, p. 29 = *Helix unguicula*, Pfr. Mon. Hel. I. p. 384.

Amboyna.

H. FLEXUOSA, Pfr. Proc. Zool. Soc. 1855, p. 112; *(Planispira)*, Pfr. Vers. p. 136; Mon. Hel. IV. p. 292.

Borneo.

H. MARTENSI, Pfr. Proc. Zool. Soc. 1861, p. 193; *(Chloritis)*, von Mart. Ostas. Zool. II. p. 279; *Planispira martensi*, Wallace, Proc. Zool. Soc. 1865, p. 409; *Helix martensi*, Pfr. Mon. Hel. V. p. 389.

Ceram.

H. UNGUICULINA, von Mart. Malak. Bl. X. 1863, p. 135; *(Chloritis)* Ostas. Zool. II. p. 278, pl. 14, fig. 5; Pfr. Mon. Hel. V. p. 390.

Buru.

H. BIOMPHALA, Pfr. Proc. Zool. Soc. 1862, p. 272; *(Chloritis)* von Martens, Ostas. Zool. II. p. 279 *Semicornu biomphalum*, Wallace, Proc. Zool. Soc. 1865, p. 410 — *Helix biomphala*, Pfr. Mon. Hel. V. p. 391.

Ceram.

H. QUADRIVOLVUS, von Mart. Monatsber. Berl. Ak. 16th Jan. 1865, p. 53; *(Chloritis)*, Ostas. Zool. II. p. 288, pl. 14, fig. 6; Pfr. Mon. Hel. V. p. 392.

Borneo.

Section 77, *Dorcasia*.

H. ARGILLACEA, (HELICOGENA), Fér. pr. 38, Hist. pl. 26, figs. 1-2; Lamarck, 53, p. 80, Dh. edit. p 50; Fér. Voy. Freycin. Zool. p. 468, pl. 67, figs. 6-7; Chemn. 2nd. edit. Helix No. 326, pl. 58, figs. 4-5 = *Galaxias argillacea*, Beck, Index, p. 42 = *Helix argillacea*, var. Fér. pl. 26, fig. 3 ; Pfr. Mon. Hel. I. p. 320.

Timor ; Rawak ; Flores.

H. TRANSVERSALIS, Mouss. Jour. Conch. VI. 1857, p. 158, pl. 6, fig. 5 ; Pfr. Mon. Hel IV. p. 350.

Bali.

Section 78, *Camaena*.

H. TRAILLI, Pfr. Proc. Zool. Soc. 1855, p. 107, pl. 32, fig. 4 ; (*Camaena*), Vers. p. 138 ; Mon. Hel. IV. p. 256.

Palawan Passage, near Borneo.

H. GERMANUS, Reeve, = *H. orientalis*, Ad. and Reeve, Voy. Samarang, Moll. p. 61, pl. 16, fig. 4 (not Gray) = *H. germanus*, Reeve, Conch. Icon. No. 385, pl. 74 ; Chemn. 2nd edit. Helix No. 925, pl. 142, figs. 1-2 ; Pfr. Mon. Hel. III. p. 222.

Borneo (?) Japan.

H. PALAWANICA, Pfr. Proc. Zool. Soc. 1855, p. 107, pl. 32, fig. 7 ; (*Camaena*), Pfr. Vers. p. 138 ; Mon. Hel. IV. p. 261.

Palawan Passage, near Borneo.

H. CONDORIANA, Crosse and Fisch. Jour. Conch. XI. 1863, p. 351, pl. 14, fig. 1 ; Pfr. Mon. Hel. V. p. 377.

Pulo Condor, Cochin-China.

Section 80, *Geotrochus*. Sub-section 1, *Geotrochi genuini*.

H. PERAKENSIS, Crosse, Jour. de Conch. XXVII. 1879, p. 199, pl. 8, fig. 4 (*Geotrochus*).

This is a small regularly conical shell, 10 millimetres in diameter and 11 high. Dr. Hungerford has some doubts about its being a *Geotrochus*, a group which has not yet been observed in the Indian region. The figure gives the idea rather of *Satsuma* (or *Fruticotrochus*, Kol.), which group is widely spread in China, and might very well range into the Malay Peninsula, hitherto so little explored. Von Moll. Jour. As. Soc. Beng. LV. 1886, p. 303.

Perak.

H. SWETTENHAMI, De Morgan, Le Naturaliste, VII. 1885, p. 68; O. von Möllendorff, Jour. As. Soc. Beng. LV. 1886, p. 304, who says the species may be a *Trochomorpha* or a *Plectotropis*. He makes the same observation with regard to the three following species :—

H. THIEROTI, De Morgan, l.c.

Gunong-Chura, north of Ipoli, Kinta Valley.

H. HARDOUINI, De Morgan, l.c.

Valley of the Kinta, between Lahat and Ipoli.

H. LAHATENSIS, De Morgan, l.c.

Same locality.

H. ANTIQUA, Ad. and Reeve, Voy. Samarang, Moll. p. 61, pl. 16, fig. 1; Reeve, Conch. Icon. No. 402, pl. 77; Chemn. 2nd edit. Helix No. 949, pl. 144, figs. 14-15; Pfr. Mon. Hel. III. p. 172.

Unsang, Borneo.

Sub-section 2, Perforati.

H. EUCHROES, Pfr. Malak. Bl. 1854, p. 57; Reeve, Conch. Icon. No. 1316, pl. 192; Pfr. Novit. Conch. I. p. 2, No. 3, pl. 1, figs. 7-8; (*Geotrochus*), Pfr. Vers. p. 145 = *Acavus euchroës* (*Geotrochus*), H. and A. Adams, Gen. II. p. 196 = *Helix euchroës*, Pfr. Mon. Hel. IV. p. 256.

Indian Archipelago.

H. LENTA, Pfr.= *H. pileus*, Pfr. Mon. Hel. I. p. 324; var. Chemn. new edit. Helix I. p. 157, pl. 40, fig. 5 = *H. lenta*, Pfr. Malak. Bl. 1854, p. 57; (*Geotrochus*), Pfr. Vers. p. 145; Mon. Hel. IV. p. 257 = *Acavus lentus* (*Geotrochus*), H. and A. Adams, Gen. II. p. 196.

Moluccas.

H. STURSIANA, Shuttlew. Bern, Mittheil. 1852, Aug. p. 200 ; Pfr. Mon. Hel. III. p. 179.

Amboyna.

H. PILEOLUS, Fér. Hist. pl. 63 A. figs. 1-2 (not Pfr. Mon. H. I. p. 324); Pfr. Malak. Bl. VII. 1860, p. 64; von Mart. Ostas. Zool. II. p. 321, pl. 17, figs. 8-9 ; Pfr. Mon. Hel. V. p. 326.

Batchian.

H. ZOAE, Pfr. Malak. Bl. XII. 1865, p. 121 ; Novit. Conch. Fasc. 23, p. 274, No. 386, pl. 67, figs. 16-17 = *H. pileolus*, Pfr. Mon. Hel. I. p. 324.

Moluccas.

H. SUBVITREA, Pfr. Proc. Zool. Soc. 1854, p. 148 ; Reeve, Conch. Icon. No. 1361, pl. 194 ; Pfr. Novit. Conch. I. p. 8, No. 13, pl. 3, figs. 8-9 : *(Geotrochus)* Pfr. Vers. p. 115.

Moluccas.

H. RHYNCHOSTOMA, Pfr. Proc. Zool. Soc. 1861, p. 21, pl. 2. fig. 6 ; Novit. Conch. p. 166, No. 264, pl. 45, figs. 9-11 ; Mon. Hel. V. p. 328.

Batchian.

H. LANCEOLATA, Pfr. Proc. Zool. Soc. 1861, p. 386, pl. 37. fig. 6 ; von Mart. Ostas. Zool. II. p. 320, pl. 17, fig. 7 ; Pfr. Mon. Hel. V. p. 328 = *Papuina lanceolata*, Wallace, Proc. Zool. Soc. 1865, p. 411.

Gilolo ; Moti.

H. NODIFERA, Pfr. Proc. Zool. Soc. 1861, p. 21, pl. 2, fig. 4 ; Novit. Conch. p. 166, No. 263, pl. 45, figs. 7-8 = *Papuina nodifera*, Wallace, Proc. Zool. Soc. 1865, p. 411 = *Helix nodifera*, Pfr. Mon. Hel. V. p. 328.

Batchian.

H. VITREA, Fér. (HELICIGONA), pr. 145, Hist. pl. 64, fig. 4 ; Chemn. 2nd edit. Helix No. 459, pl. 76, figs. 18-19 ; Pfr. Mon. Hel. I. p. 326.

Ternate ; Moti ; Batchian.

H. ALBULA, Le Guill. Revue Zool. 1842, p. 139 ; Pfr. Mon. Hel. I. p. 328.

Ternate.

Sub-section 3, Pseudopartula.

H. (BULIMUS) GALERICULUM, Mouss. (Pfr. Nomenclator Hel. p. 197, No. 83) = *Bulimus galericulum*, Mouss. Jav. Moll. p. 34, pl. 3, fig. 5 ; Pfr. Mon. Hel. III. p. 302.

Pardana, Java.

Section 5, Corasia.

H. EXTENSA, Müll. Verm. II. p. 60, No. 254 (not Fér.); Gmel. Syst. p. 3631, No. 59; Lamarck, Hist. VI. p. 70, No. 18, Desh. edit. VIII. p. 37 ; Desh. in Fér. Hist. I. p. 246, No. 313, pl. 96, figs. 5-7 ; Chemn. 2nd edit. Helix No. 1090, pl. 160, figs. 6-7 ; Pfr. Mon. Hel. III. p. 192 = *Eurycratera extensa*, Beck, Ind. p. 46, No. 9.

Amboyna ; Goram.

H. LEUCOPHTHALMA, Pfr. Malak. Bl. XVII. 1870, p. 93 ; Novit. Conch. IV. p. 10, No. 681, pl. 111, figs. 8-9 = *Cochlostyla* (*Corasia*) *leucophthalma*, Paetel, Catal. 1873, p. 97 ; = *Helix leucophthalma*, Pfr. Mon. Hel. VII. p. 355.

Celebes.

H. LAIS, Pfr. Proc. Zool. Soc. 1853; Mon. Hel. III. p. 647. Island of Tukan Bessi.

H. COCHLOSTYLA, Fér. Prodromus, p. 47, Sub-genus of *Helix*.

Shell not umbilicated, oval, conical, ventricose, somewhat like a *Bulimus* with rather obtuse apex. Aperture large, ovate ; columella straight or slightly curved ; peristome reflected. About 214 species, generally characteristic of the Philippines and Indian Archipelago, some in India, others in Cochin China, while a few extend into the Pacific as far as Fiji and New Caledonia. (?)

COCHLOSTYLA THOMSONI, Pfr. Nomen. Hel. p. 205, No. 2116 = *Helix thomsoni*, Pfr. Malak. Bl. XVIII. 1871, p. 120; Novit. Conch. IV. p. 70, No. 756, pl. 121, figs. 1-2 = *Cochlostyla thomsoni (Corasia)*, Paetel, Catal. 1873, p. 97 = *Helix thomsoni*, Pfr. Mon. Hel. VII. p. 308.

Island of Tukan Bessi.

C. INDUSIATA, Pfr. Nomencl. Hel. p. 205, No. 2489 = *Helix indusiata*, Pfr. Malak. Bl. XVIII. 1871, p. 121; Novit. Conch. IV. p. 71, No. 757, p. 121, figs. 3-4; Mon. Hel. VII. p. 355.

Tukan Bessi.

C. RUSTICA, Mouss. = *Bulimus rusticus*, Mouss. Jav. Moll. 115, pl. 22, fig. 1; Reeve, Conch. Icon. No. 574, pl. 78; Pfr. Mon. Hel. III. p. 296 = *Cochlostyla rustica*, Pfr. Nomen. Hel. p. 208, No. 17.

Java.

C. TRAILLI, Pfr. = *Bulimus trailli*, Pfr. Proc. Zool. Soc. 1856, p. 106, pl. 32, fig. 6; *(Amphidromus)*, Pfr. Vers. p. 146; Mon. Hel. IV. p. 362.

Borneo.

C. PALAWANENSIS, Pfr. = *Bulimus palawanensis*, Pfr. Mon. Hel. IV. p. 372.

Palawan.

C. LIBROSA, Pfr. = *Bulimus librosus*, Pfr. Proc. Zool. Soc. 1856, p. 388; Mon. Hel. IV. p. 375.

Palawan.

12. BULIMUS, Scopoli, Deliciæ Floræ et Faunæ Insubricæ. (Lombardy) Vol. I. p. 67.

Shell oval, oblong, or turriculate, solid, sub-perforate or imperforate; whorls few; ultimate ventricose wide; aperture longitudinal; columella broad, rarely plicate; peristome thickened, reflected; margins usually joined by a callus.

Animal similar to the animal of *Helix*, with a simple jaw.*

Radula similar also to *Helix*. Between 300 and 400 species, mostly South American.†

---

* It cannot be questioned that Scopoli rather than Adanson should be given as the authority for this genus, although the author of the work referred to in the text says distinctly, " Proprium itaque ex his constituo, et duce celeberrimo Adansonio Buli*mos* voco, ut eo facilius adnoscantur. Solam testam nec animal inhabitans vidi, quod diversum esse à Limace affirmat Adansonius." p. 67.

Cf. Histoire Naturelle du Sénégal (Paris, 1757), where M. Adanson writes the name Bulin. The Latin(?) name on pl. 1 looks very much like Bulimus in consequence of the strokes of the "n" and "u" being confused. A brief account of this curious work may be useful. It is divided into two parts; the first of 190 pages is devoted to the "Voyage au Sénégal;" the second part is a "Histoire des Coquillages," consisting of :— 1. Préface, 28 pp.; 2. Définitions des parties des coquillages, 32 pp. (a most useful series of observations well deserving of study); 3. Table des rapports ou des combinaisons autrement appellés systèmes ou arrangements méthodiques, 26 pp.; 4. Table chronologique des auteurs, 4 pp.; 5. Division générale, 4 pp.; 6. Coquillages (including index), 275 pp.; 7. Plates, 19 pp. At p. 5 of the Coquillages is a full description which extends to three pages of Le Bulin or Bulinus, from which only the first sentence need be cited, as it shows the author is dealing with a fresh-water shell. " Je donne le nom de Bulin à un petit coquillage d' eau douce, qui vit communément sur la lentille de marais et sur le lemna, dans les marais et les étangs de Podor." Therefore Scopoli's genus, spelled differently, is justly regarded as new.

† It is a curious feature in the Philippine and some of the Malay species that the varieties of pattern, which constitute their chief ornament, reside only in the epidermis. The colours of the shell rarely describe any sort of configuration; they are mostly blended into a uniform tint, over which a fanciful pattern is produced by the epidermis forming a double porous membrane in some places, and a single one only in others, developed, moreover, with the same continuous regularity as the textile marking of a Volute or Cone. This phenomenon is easily detected by immersing the shell in water, when the light portion or upper porous layer of epidermis becomes saturated, and the ground color of the shell is seen through it; as the moisture evaporates, the epidermis resumes its light appearance. Sir David Brewster, in reply to a letter from Mr. Broderip on this subject, says : " It appears to me, from very careful observations, that the epidermis consists of two layers, and that it is only the upper layer which is porous wherever the pattern is white. These white or porous portions of the

Section Amphidromus.

BULIMUS LORICATUS, Pfr.   Proc. Zool. Soc. 1854, p. 293; (*Amphidromus*) Pfr. Vers. p. 147 ; Mon. Hel. IV. p. 372.

Java.

B. PERVERSUS, L.= *Helix perversa*, L. Syst. Nat. 12th edit. Species, No. 136. Sub-umbilicate, ovate, oblong, often sinistral, colour various, but generally uniformly light green, lemon yellow, or white ; or marked variously with spots or bands, such as a deep brown oblique streak, white with red spot, red lip, white lip, variously spotted with a bluish throat. This well-known and widely-spread shell which is found all through the Archipelago (Borneo?), Malay Peninsula, Moluccas and Burmah, was known to the early conchologists, twelve authorities being quoted by Linnæus for this species and *B. dextra*, which is evidently a variety. It is unnecessary to reproduce the authorities which occupy nearly two pages of Pfeiffer's Mon. Hel. (Vol. III. p. 308). It is very common about Malacca, and on wet days especially may be gathered off the leaves of the trees where it is with difficulty distinguished on account of the similarity of its colour. Without quoting authorities, it may be mentioned that it has been known by the following names :—*Bulimus, Helix, Limax, Orthostylus, perversa, dextra, sinistra, atricallosa, interrupta, aurea, citrina, sultana, javanica, macassariensis*.

B. LEUCOXANTHUS, von Mart. *B. leucoxanthus*, von Mart. Monatsber. Berl. Ak. 18th July, 1864, p. 526 (Reeve, Bul. f. 187 b : dextra.) ; Ostas. Zool. II. p. 348, pl. 20, figs. 11-12 (sinistr.) ; Pfr. Mon. Hel. VI. p. 18.

Java.

---

epidermis differ from the other parts of the upper layer only in having been deprived of, or in never having possessed, the element which gives transparency to the membrane ; in the same manner as hydrophanous opal has become white, from the expulsion of its water of crystallization." Reeve, Conch. Icon. Bulimus.

B. POLYMORPHUS (COCHLOSTYLA), Tapp. Canefri *Cochlostyla polymorpha*, Tapp. Canefri, Malac. del viaggio della fregata Magenta, 1874, p. 82, pl. 2, figs. 4 a-b. = *Bulimus polymorphus*, Pfr. Mon. Hel. VIII. p. 23. M. H. Crosse (Jour. Conch. 1874, p. 320) regards this species as only a variety of *B. (Amphidromus) comes*, Pfr. of Cambodia.

Singapore.

B. MELANOMMA, Pfr. = *Helix flammea*, Chemn. IX. p. 94, fig. 927 = *Bulimus inversus*, Küst. pl. 6, fig. 3 (ex Chemn.) *B. citrinus*, var. Reeve, Conch. Icon. pl. 31, fig. 187a = *B. elongatus*, Hombr. et Jacq. Voy. Pole Sud, Moll. pl. 8, figs. 3-4 (?) = *B. melanomma*. Pfr. Zeitsch. f. Malak. 1852, p. 95 ; Chemn. 2nd edit. Bul. No. 179, pl. 39, figs. 28-29 ; Pfr. Mon. Hel. III. p. 310.

Singapore ; Borneo.

B. LINSTEDTI, Pfr. Proc. Zool. Soc. 1856, p. 388 ; Mon. Hel. IV. p. 374.

Malacca.

B. MUNDUS, Pfr. Zeitschr. f. Malak. 1853, p. 57 ; Mon. Hel. III. p. 651 ; Chemn. 2nd edit. Bul. p. 373, pl. 70, figs. 21-22.

Singapore.

B. BATAVLE (PARTULA), Grateloup, = *Partula bataviæ*, Grat. Act. Bord. XI. p. 425, pl. 2, fig. 12 = *Bulimus bataviæ*, Pfr. Mon. Hel. II. p. 40.

Java.

B. INVERSUS, Müll. = *B. inversus*, Mouss. Jav. Moll. p. 107 ; Pfr. Zeitschr. f. Malak. 1849, p. 132 ; *(Amphidromus)* Albers, Helic. p. 138 ; *(Helix)* Pfr. Mon. Hel. III. p. 318.

This has been as long known as *Bulimus perversus*, and has had the same synonyms applied to it.

Malacca ; Singapore ; Siam.

B. winteri, Pfr. Zeitschr. f. Malak. 1849, p. 135; Chemn. 2nd edit. Bul. No. 177, pl. 40, figs. 3-4; Pfr. Mon. Hel. III. p. 319.

Java.

B. teysmanni, Mouss. MSS.; Pfr. Novit. Conch. IV. p. 32, No. 704, pl. 116, figs. 2-3; Mon. Hel. VIII. p. 40 = *B. winteri*, von Mart. Ostas. II. p. 353.

Moluccas.

B. heerianus, Mouss. MSS.; Pfr. Novit. Conch. IV. p. 31, No. 703, pl. 116, fig. 4 = *B. winteri* var. von Mart. Ostas. Moll. pl. 20, fig. 10 (?) = *B. heerianus*, Pfr. Mon. Hel. VIII. p. 40.

Moluccas.

B. palaceus, v. d. Busch, in litt; Mouss. Jav. Moll. p. 28, pl. 3, fig. 1; Pfr. Zeitschr. f. Malak. 1849, p. 136; Mon. Hel. III. p. 320; Chemn. 2nd edit. Bul. No. 178, pl. 40, fig. 6; (*Amphidromus*), Alb. Helic. p. 138 = *B. perversus*, Pfr. Mon. Hel. II. p. 37.

Java.

B. purus, Mouss. Jav. Moll. p. 29, pl. 3, fig. 2; Pfr. Novit. Conch. IV. p. 33, No. 705, pl. 116, fig. 6 = *B. palaceus*, Pfr. Mon. Hel. III. p. 320 = *B. winteri*, von Mart. Ostas. Moll. p. 354, ex parte = *B. purus*, Pfr. Mon. Hel. VIII. p. 41.

Java.

B. emaciatus (Amphidromus), von Mart. Ostas. Zool. II. p. 347, pl. 20, fig. 7; Pfr. Mon. Hel. VI. p. 25.

Java; Bali.

B. appressus, Mouss. in coll.; Pfr. Mon. Hel. VI. p. 26, No. 213b. (ex v. Mart.); (*Amphidromus*) von Mart. Ostas. Moll. p. 353; Pfr. Novit. Conch. IV. p. 34, No. 706, pl. 116, figs. 4-5; Mon. Hel. VIII. p. 42.

Java.

B. lævus, Müll. = *Helix læva*, Müll. Verm. II. p. 95, No. 293; Chemn. IX. P. I, p. 103, pl. 111, figs. 940-49; Gmel. p. 3641,

No. 100; Dillw. Descr. Cat. II. p. 935, No. 112; (*Cochlogena*) Fér. pr. 416 = *H. perversa*, Gmel. p. 3643 (e fig. Kämm.) = *Bulimus lævus*, Brug. Enc. Méth. I. p. 317, No. 31; Quoy et Gaim. Astrol. II. p. 120, pl. 10, fig. 4; Lamarck, Desh. edit. 80, p. 260; Küster, p. 15, pl. 9, figs. 7-16 *Orthostylus lævus*, Beck, Ind. p. 50, No. 15; Kämmerer, p. 125, pl. 10, fig. 3 = *B. lævus*, Pfr. Mon. Hel. II. p. 39.

Timor.

B. SUSPECTUS, von Mart. Monatsber. Berl. Ak. 18th July, 1864, p. 526; Ostas. Zool. II. p. 362, pl. 21, fig. 8; Pfr. Mon. Hel. VI. p. 27.

Kupang, Timor.

B. SUMATRANUS, von Mart. Monatsber. Berl. Ak. 18th July, 1864, p. 526; Ostas. Zool. II. p. 366, pl. 21, fig. 6; Pfr. Mon. Hel. VI. p. 27.

Sumatra.

B. SINISTRALIS, Reeve, Conch. Icon. No. 603, pl. 81; Chemn. 2nd edit. Bul. No. 181, pl. 41, figs. 11-13 = *B. lævus*, var Desh. in Fér. Hist. pl. 161, figs. 11, 14-18 = *B. sinistralis*, Pfr. Mon. Hel. III. p. 321.

Celebes; Timor.

B. CONTRARIUS, Müller, = *Helix contrarius*, Müll. Verm. II. p. 95, No. 292 (Swamm. pl. 7, No. 11); Gmel. Syst. p. 3644, No. 99; Fer. Voy. Freyc. p. 474, pl. 67, figs. 8-9 = *H. interrupta sinistrorsa*, Chemn. IX. p. 101, figs. 938-939 = *Bulimus contrarius*, Pfr. Mon. Hel. III. p. 327.

Macassar; Timor; Java.

B. PORCELLANUS, Mouss. Jav. Moll. p. 33, pl. 3, fig. 4; (*Amphidromus*), Alb. Helic. p. 139; Chemn. 2nd edit. Bul. No. 182, pl. 41, figs. 14-15; Pfr. Mon. Hel. III. p. 328.

Java.

B. ADAMSII, Reeve, Conch. Icon. No. 73, pl. 13; Adams and Reeve, Voy. Samarang, Moll. p. 58, pl. 15, fig. 1; Chemn. 2nd edit. Bul. No. 105, pl. 31, figs. 11-12; Pfr. Nomen. Hel. p. 214, No. 300.

Borneo.

Family BULIMINIDA.

13. BULIMINA, Ehren. Symb. Phys. Oken Isis, 1833, p. 734, sub-genus, *Chilodontis*.

Shell solid, rimate, oblong conical, or fusiformly cylindrical; apex obtuse, horny, last whorl shorter than spire; aperture small, oblique, oval; peristome straight, labiate within, simple or dentate; lip rather expanded, columella reflexed and spread.

Animal similar to *Bulimus*, jaw arcuate and finely striate lengthwise; radula like *Helix*. About 350 species, which are divided into about a dozen sub-genera, of which four only belong to America or about an eighth of the species; the rest are in Europe and western Asia, with a few extending into the Indian Archipelago, belonging as far as known to the sub-genus *Ena*.

BULIMINA LORRAINI, Pfr. = *Bulimus lorraini*, Pfr. Proc. Zool. Soc. 1856, p. 332; Mon Hel. IV. p. 468.

Penang.

B. SPILOZONA, von Mart. = *Bulimus* (*Rhachis*) *spilozonus*, von Mart. Monatsber. Berl. Ak. 18th July, 1864, p. 527; Ostas. Zool. II. p. 368, pl. 21, fig. 13; Pfr. Mon. Hel VI. p. 112.

Celebes; Timor.

B. GREGARIA, Ad. and Reeve, = *Bulimus gregarius*, Ad. and Reeve, Voy. Samarang, Moll. p. 58, pl. 14, fig. 4; Reeve, Conch. Icon. No. 612, pl. 83 (aliquantulum auct.); Pfr. Mon. Hel. III. p. 351.

Borneo; Japan.

B. GLANDULA, Mouss. = *Bulimus glandulus*, Mouss. Jav. Moll. p. 34, pl. 4, fig. 3; Pfr. Mon. Hel. III. p. 353.

Java.

B. APERTA, von Mart. = *Pupa aperta*, von Mart. Malak. Bl. X. 1863, p. 180 = *Buliminus apertus* (*Napaeus*), von Mart. Ostas. Zool. II. 370, pl. 22, fig. 6 = *Bulimus apertus*, Pfr. Mon. Hel. VI. p. 61.

Timor.

14. STENOGYRA, Shuttleworth, Diagnosis Nov. Moll. No. 6.
p. 137.

Shell elongate, turriculate ; whorls numerous ; apex obtuse or truncate ; aperture oval, small ; columella thin, straight ; peristome simple, sharp.

Animal like *Achatina*. Jaw finely plicate or ribbed ; radula with median tooth, very small ; laterals tricuspid with a rather long central cusp ; marginals short, tricuspid. About 250 species, of world-wide distribution. The species of the Malayan region belong to the section *Opeas*, in which the shell is small, thin, subulate, covered with small ribs.

STENOGYRA GRACILIS, Hutton, Jour. As. Soc. Beng. III. p. 84 = *Bulimus gracilis*, Hutton, l.c. = *B. indicus*, Pfr. Mon. Hel. II. p. 157 ; Chemn. pl. 21, figs. 18-19 = *B. apex*, Mouss. = *Spiraxis gracilis*, Blanford, Contrib. Ind. Malac. = *Bulimus cereus*, Reeve, Conch. Icon. Achatina, pl. 17, fig. 81.

Java ; Bukit Pondok, Perak.

S. (SUBULINA) TCHEHELENSIS, De Morgan, Le Naturaliste, 1885, p. 69 = *S.* (*Opeas*) *terebralis* (?), Theobald (? n.sp.), G. Nevill, Handl. Moll. Ind. Mus. 1878, p. 166 ; O. F. von Möllendorff, Jour. As. Soc. Beng. LV. p. 304.

This is a fine subulate shell, more than an inch long with 10 or 12 whorls.

Mount Chehel, near the River Plus and Bukit Pondok, Perak.

S. ARCTISPIRA (OPEAS), von Mart. Ostas. Zool. II. p. 374. pl. 22, fig. 10 = *Bulimus arctispirus*, Pfr. Mon. Hel. VI. p. 102.

Java.

S. DENSESPIRATA, Mouss. = *Bulimus densespiratus*, Mouss. Jour. Conch. VI. 1857, p. 159; Pfr. Mon. Hel. IV. p. 497.

Buitenzorg, Java.

S. ACUTISSIMA, Mouss. = *Bulimus acutissimus*, Mouss. Jour. Conch. VI. 1857, p. 159; Pfr. Mon. Hel. IV. p. 453.

Buitenzorg, Java.

S. LAXISPIRA, von Mart. Ostas. Zool. II. p. 373, pl. 22, fig. 14 = *Bulimus laxispirus*, Pfr. Mon. Hel. VI. p. 92.

Sumatra.

S. HOCHSTETTERI, Zelebor, — *Bulimus hochstetteri*, Zeleb. Reise der Freg. "Novara;" Pfr. Mon. Hel. VI. p. 107.

Java.

S. ACHATINACEA, Pfr. — *Bulimus achatinaceus*, Pfr. Symb. III. p. 82; Mon. Hel. II. p. 156.

Java; Borneo.

15. RHODINA, De Morgan, Le Naturaliste, 1885, p. 68.

Shell cylindraceous, striate; whorls numerous, last much larger; aperture triangular; columella reflected, very prominent; peristome continuous.

M. de. Morgan has founded this new genus for a curious shell like *Stenogyra*. He thinks it is related to *Rhodea* by the absence of keel and the cornet-like aperture.

RHODINA PERAKENSIS, De Morgan, l.c.

Shell cylindrical, fragile, horny, yellow, with 10 regularly increasing whorls very regularly and distinctly striate, the suture linear and well marked; the aperture triangular, oblique; peristome thin, not reflected.

Long. 25, diam. of last whorl $4\frac{1}{2}$, long. of aperture 5, lat. 3 mill.

Limestone rocks of Gunong Tcheura, near Ipoli, Kinta Valley, under dead leaves.

Family CIONELLIDA.

16. GLESSULA, Albers, Helic. p. 194.

Shell ovate, oblong; thin translucent; spire pyramidal; apex obtuse; whorls numerous, last inflated; columella short, arcuate, abruptly truncate.

Fifty-nine species in India, Malayan region, and West Africa.

GLESSULA WALLACEI, Pfr.=*Achatina wallacei* (*Electra*), Pfr. Malak. Bl. 1855, p. 168; Novit. Conch. I. p. 82, No. 140, pl. 22, figs. 9-10; Mon. Hel. IV. p. 606.

Sarawak, Borneo.

G. SUMATRANA, von Mart.= *Achatina sumatrana*, von Mart. Ostas. Zool. II. pl. 22, fig. 5. *Cionella sumatrana*, von Mart. Monats. Berl. Ak. 18th July, 1864, p. 527 =*Achatina sumatrana*, Pfr. Mon. Hel. VI. p. 225.

Sumatra.

G. JAVANICA, Reeve,= *Achatina javanica*, Reeve, Conch. Icon. No. 79, pl. 17; Pfr. Mon. Hel. III. p. 493.

Java.

Family PUPIDA.

17. PUPA, Lamarck, Syst. Anim. s. Vert. 1st edit. p. 88.

Shell usually very small, cylindrical or oval oblong; umbilicus slight or a mere slit, striate, plicate or ribbed, brown or horn-colour; columella plaited or sub-dentate; lip reflected, dentate or plaited within; peristome joined usually by a callosity.

Animal with a short foot, pointed behind, lower tentacles short; jaw smooth or finely striated, often with a superior appendage like *Succinea*.

Radula resembling *Helix*; the central and lateral teeth similar, tricuspid; marginals very short and denticulated.

Pupa ascendens, von Mart. Monatsber. Berl. Ak. 18th July, 1864, p. 528; (*Anostomella*), Ostas. Zool. II. p. 386, pl. 22, fig. 23; Pfr. Mon. Hel. VI. p. 297.

Amboyna.

P. orcella (Pupisoma), Stol. Jour. As. Soc. Beng. XLII. 1873, p. 33, pl. 3, fig. 2; Pfr. Mon. Hel. VIII. p. 358.

Penang.

P. moreleti, A. D. Brown, Jour. Conch. XVIII. 1870, p. 393 = *Vertigo moreleti*, Issel, Moll. Born. p. 52 = *Pupa moreleti*, Pfr. Mon. Hel. VIII. p. 391.

Labuan.

P. malayana, Issel,— *Vertigo malayanus*, Issel, Moll. Born. 1874, p. 53, pl. 5, figs. 30-32 — *Pupa malayana* (*Vertigo*), Pfr. Mon. Hel. VIII. p. 104.

Borneo.

P. palmira (Scopelophila), Stol. Jour. As. Soc. Beng. XLII. 1873, p. 32; Pfr. Mon. Hel. VIII. p. 109.

Penang.

18. Hypselostoma, Benson.

Ann. and Magaz. Nat. Hist. 1856, Feb. p. 130, also, Ap. p. 342; H. and A. Adams, Gen. II. p. 640. = *Tanystoma*, Benson, l.c.

Shell convolute, conical, perforate, last whorl free, opening upwards, protracted; aperture trumpet-like and dentate; peristome horizontal, expanded.

Three species collected in Burmah.

Hypselostoma bensonianum, W. Blanford, Contr. Ind. Mal. IV. 1863, p. 8; Pfr. Mon. Hel. V. 1868, p. 137; Conch. Indica, pl. 8, fig. 2; von Möll. Jour. As. Soc. Beng. LV. 1886, p. 306.

Perak.

19. CLAUSILIA, Draparnaud, Hist. Nat. d. Moll. terrest. et fluv. pp. 24, 29, 68.

Shell fusiform, usually sinistral ; aperture elliptical or pyriform with a posterior sinus contracted by lamellæ closed when adult by a moveable shelly plate (*Clausilium*) ; peristome continuous, reflected.

Animal with a short obtuse foot ; upper tentacles short, lower small ; lung and reproductive orifices on the left side ; jaw finely grooved.

Radula like *Helix*, but both rows very numerous, sometimes as many as 120×50. About 700 species, of world-wide distribution. The peculiarity of the genus is the *Clausilium*, which is developed in the adult state. The animal secretes an elastic calcareous filament attached to the columella, round which it makes a half turn. At the free end is a spoon-shaped lamina, smaller than the aperture, but fitting it. Its elasticity enables the animal to push it on one side when walking, and to use it as a door when within the shell, securing it against intrusion.

CLAUSILIA MOLUCCENSIS, von Mart. Monatsber. Berl. Ak. Apr. 1864, p. 270 ; (*Phaedusa*), Ostas. Zool. II. p. 381, pl. 22, fig. 19 ; Pfr. Mon. Hel. VI. p. 412.

Halmahera ; Ternate.

CL. PENANGENSIS (PHAEDUSA), Stol. Jour. As. Soc. Beng. XLII. 1873, p. 27, pl. 3, figs. 4-6 ; Pfr. Mon. Hel. VIII. p. 465.

Penang Hill.

CL. SUMATRANA, von Mart. Monatsber. Berl. Ak. April, 1864, p. 270 ; (*Phaedusa*), Ostas. Zool. II. p. 379, pl. 22, fig. 17 ; Pfr. Mon. Hel. VI. p. 410.

Sumatra.

CL. HELDII, Küst. p. 27, pl. 2, figs. 29-31 = *Cl. javana*, Pfr. Mon. Hel. II. p. 405.

Java.

CL. JAVANA, Pfr. Symb. I. p. 49; Küst. p. 26, pl. 1, figs. 26-28 = *Cl. heldii*, Küst. p. 27, pl. 2, figs. 29-31 = *Cl. javana*, Pfr. Mon. Hel. II. p. 405.

Java.

CL. CORTICINA, v. d. Busch, MSS.; Pfr. Symb. II. p. 60; Küst. p. 26, pl. 2, figs. 24-25; Pfr. Mon. Hel. II. p. 404.

Java.

CL. BORNEENSIS, Pfr. Proc. Zool. Soc. 1854, p. 296; (*Phaedusa*), Pfr. Vers. p. 181; Mon. Hel. IV. p. 736.

Borneo.

CL. JUNGHUHNI, Phil. in Küst. Mon. p. 23, pl. 2, figs. 5-7; Pfr. Mon. Hel. II. p. 405.

Java.

CL. CORNEA, Phil. in Küst. Mon. p. 22, pl. 2, figs. 1-4; Pfr. Mon. Hel. II. p. 405.

Java.

CL. EXCURRENS, von Mart. Monatsber. Berl. Ak. 18th July, 1864, p. 527; Ostas. Zool. II. p. 384, pl. 22, fig. 16; Pfr. Mon. Hel. VI. p. 480.

Kepahiang, Sumatra.

CL. FILICOSTATA (PHAEDUSA), Stol. Jour. As. Soc. Beng. XLII. 1873, p. 28, pl. 3, figs. 7-8; Pfr. Mon. Hel. VIII. p. 471.

Penang Hill.

CL. OBESA (PHAEDUSA), von Mart. Ostas. Zool. II. p. 380 (not Pfr.) = *Cl. obesa*, Pfr. Mon. Hel. VI. p. 411.

Indian Archipelago.

CL. ORIENTALIS, v.d. Busch, MSS.; Pfr. Symb. II. p. 60; Küst. p. 25, pl. 2, figs. 17-19; Pfr. Mon. Hel. II. p. 414.

Java.

CL. SCHWANERI, Herklots, Mus. Lugd. Bat.; (*Phaedusa*), von Mart. Ostas. Zool. II. p. 382; Pfr. Mon. Hel. VI. p. 468.

Borneo.

Cl. (Pseudonenia) filicostata, Stol. Jour. As. Soc. Beng. XLII. 1873, p. 28, pl. 3, figs. 7-8 ; var. *tenuicosta*, G. Nevill, Handl. Moll. Ind. Mus. 1878, p. 183 ; H. Crosse, Jour. Conch. XXVII. 1879, p. 337 ; O. F. von Möll. Jour. As. Soc. Beng. LV. 1886, p. 306.

Bukit Pondok, Perak.

" The few badly preserved specimens which Dr. Hungerford found seem to justify Nevill's classification of the Perak form as a variety of the Penang *Cl. filicostata*." O. F. von Möll. l.c.

Family SUCCINEIDEA.

The shells of this family are thin, horny, oval, oblong ; spire only slightly developed, mouth very wide, oval ; columella simple not truncate, peristome with a thin edge.

20. Succinea, Draparnaud, Tableau Moll. pp. 32, 55.

Shell imperforate, thin, ovate or oblong ; spire small ; aperture large, obliquely oval ; columella and peristome simple, acute.

Animal large, tentacles short and thick, foot broad ; lingual teeth like *Helix*. Inhabits damp places, but rarely enters the water.

Succinea borneensis, Pfr. Proc. Zool. Soc. 1851 ; Mon. Hel. III. p. 11.

Borneo.

S. taylori, Pfr. Proc. Zool. Soc. 1851 ; Mon. Hel. III. p. 10.

Singapore.

S. subrugata, Pfr. Proc. Zool. Soc. 1851 ; Mon. Hel. III. p. 10.

Borneo.

S. obesa, von Mart. Ostas. Zool. II. p. 387, pl. 22, fig. 21 ; Pfr. Mon. Hel. V. p. 463.

East Java.

S. GRACILIS, Lea, Proc. Amer. Phil. Soc. 1841, II. p. 31; Pfr. Mon. Hel. II. p. 518.

Java (?).

S. MINUTA, Mouss. Zolling. in Peterm. Geog. Mittheil. 1864, H. VIII. p. 303 (Nomen); Mart. Ostas. Zool. II. p. 388; Pfr. Mon. Hel. V. p. 464.

Bali.

Family CYCLOPHORIDÆ.

The Cyclophoridæ have heliciform shells with a circular opening, and covered with a thick periostraca; operculum calcareous or horny, spiral with numerous whorls.

Animal with long, slender, pointed tentacles, foot broadly expanded, not grooved.

21. CYCLOTUS, Guilding.

Conchological Papers, by L. Guilding. See Swainson, "Shells and Shell-fish," pp. 182 and 336.

Shell nearly discoid; pillar none; spire scarcely raised; lip thickened; widely umbilicate; operculum shelly; whorls numerous with raised margins. 44 species, mostly tropical.

CYCLOTUS HUNGERFORDIANUS, O. von Möll. Jour. As. Soc. Beng. LV. 1886, p. 306.

Bukit Pondok, Perak.

C. (?) DISCOIDEUS, Sowerby = *Cyclostoma discoideum*, Sow. Thes. N. 60, p. 111, pl. 25, figs. 87-88; Chemn. 2nd edit. Cycl. No. 153, p. 144, pl. 20, figs. 1-3; Mouss. Jav. Moll. p. 50, pl. 20, fig. 10 *Aperostoma discoideum*, Pfr. in Zeitschr. f. Malak. 1847, p. 104 — *Cyclotus discoideus*, Gray, Catal. Cycloph. p. 8, No. 11; Pfr. Consp. No. 36; Mon. Pneumon. Viv. p. 36.

Malang, Java.

C. OPALINUS, Mouss. — *Cyclostoma opalinum*, Mouss. Jav. Moll. p. 51, pl. 5, fig. 12 — *Cyclotus opalinus*, Pfr. Consp. No. 37; Mon. Pneumon. p. 36.

Malang, Java.

C. CORNICULUM, Mouss. = *Cyclostoma corniculum*, Mouss. Jav. Moll. p. 51, pl. 5, fig. 11 = *Cyclotus corniculum*, Pfr. Consp. No. 40; Mon. Pneumon. p. 38.

Pardana, Java.

C. TAYLORIANUS, Pfr. = *Cyclostoma taylorianum*, Pfr. Zeitschr. f. Malak. 1851, p. 7; Chemn. 2nd edit. Cycl. No. 285, pl. 38, figs. 27-29, pl. 43, figs. 1-3 = *Cyclotus taylorianum*, Pfr. Mon. Pneumon. p. 40.

Sarawak, Borneo.

C. ROSTELLATUS, Pfr. = *Cyclostoma rostellatum*, Pfr. Zeitschr. f. Malak. 1851, p. 8; Chemn. 2nd edit. Cycl. No. 286, pl. 38, figs. 30-34 = *Cyclotus rostellatus*, Pfr. Mon. Pneumon. p. 40.

Singapore.

C. LINDSTEDTI, Pfr. = *Cyclostoma lindstedti (Cyclotus)*, Pfr. Proc. Zool. Soc. 1856, p. 391 = *Cyclotus lindstedti*, Pfr. Mon. Pneumon. Suppl. I. p. 24.

Mount Ophir, Malacca.

C. PTYCHORAPHE, von Mart. Monatsber. Berl. Ak. 25 Feb. 1864; Pfr. Mon. Pneumon. Suppl. II. p. 15.

Borneo.

C. (?) PARVULUS, von Mart. Malak. Bl. X. 1863, p. 85; Pfr. Mon. Pneumon. Suppl. II. p. 17.

Ternate; Tidore.

C. RETICULATUS, von Mart. Monatsber. Berl. Ak. 25 Feb. 1864; Pfr. Mon. Pneumon. Suppl. II. p. 17.

Timor; Flores; Adenare and Solor.

C. SUCCINCTUS, von Mart. Monatsber. Berl. Ak. 25 Feb. 1864; Pfr. Mon. Pneumon. Suppl. II. p. 17.

Timor.

C. LIRATULUS, von Mart. Monatsber. Berl. Ak. 25 Feb. 1864; Pfr. Mon. Pneumon. Suppl. II. p. 27.

Moluccas.

C. BICARINATUS, von Mart. Monatsber. Berl. Ak. 25 Feb. 1864; Pfr. Mon. Pneumon. Suppl. II. p. 27.

Ceram.

C. CARINULATUS, von Mart. Monatsber. Berl. Ak. 25 Feb. 1864; Pfr. Mon. Pneumon. Suppl. II. p. 28.

Buru.

C. PRUINOSUS, von Mart. Malak. Bl. X. 1863, p. 83; Pfr. Mon. Pneumon. Suppl. II. p. 34.

Animal black. Common in the islands of Molucca, Ternate, Tidore, and Moti.

C. BATCHIANENSIS, Pfr. Proc. Zool. Soc. 1861, p. 28, pl. 3, fig. 1; Mon. Pneumon. Suppl. II. p. 35; Reeve, Conch. Icon. sp. 46, pl. 8.

Batchian.

C. LATISTRIGUS, von Mart. Monatsber. Berl. Ak. 25 Feb. 1864; Pfr. Mon. Pneumon. Suppl. II. p. 35.

Borneo.

C. FASCIATUS, von Mart., Monatsber. Berl. Ak. 25 Feb. 1864; Pfr. Mon. Pneumon. Suppl. II. p. 35.

Celebes.

C. FULMINULATUS, von Mart. Monatsber. Berl. Ak. 16 Jan. 1865, p. 21; Pfr. Mon. Pneumon. Suppl. III. p. 27 = *Cyclotus politus*, von Mart. Malak. Bl. XI. 1864, p. 141 (not Sowerby).

Celebes.

C. LONGIPILUS, von Mart. Monatsber. Berl. Ak. 16 Jan. 1865, p. 51; Pfr. Mon. Pneumon. Suppl. III. p. 28.

Maros, Celebes.

C. AMBOINENSIS (CYCLOSTOMA), Pfr. Mon. Pneumon. Suppl. III. p. 32; von Mart. Ostas. Zool. II. p. 121, pl. 2, figs. 4-5 = *Cyclostoma amboinense*, Pfr. 1852, = (?) *Cyclophorus amboinensis*, Pfr. Mon. Pneumon. p. 82, No. 49 = *Cyclophorus marmoratus*, Fér. Pfr. Mon. Pneumon. p. 68 (Martens).

Amboyna; Ceram; Buru.

22. OPISTHOPORUS, Benson.

Zeitschr. f. Malak. 1851, p. 8; Pfr. Mon. Pneumon. Viv. Suppl. III. p. 41; Zeitschr. f. Malak. 1851, p. 8; Pfr. Mon. Pneumon. Viv. Suppl. I. p. 25, II. p. 36.

Shell depressed, orbicular, largely umbilicate; aperture double, with the external parts spread out; suture behind the opening and furnished with a little open tube; operculum calcareous, circular, rather thick, concave at both sides, multispiral, double; the internal side covered with a horny periostraca, the external calcareous and rough; columella margin concave.

OPISTHOPORUS SOLUTUS, Stol. Jour. As. Soc. Beng. XLI. 1872, p. 266, pl. 10, figs. 8-10; Pfr. Mon. Pneumon. Suppl. III. 1876, p. 44; G. Nevill, Handl. Moll. Ind. Mus. 1878, p. 263; H. Crosse, Jour. Conch. XXVII. 1879, p. 337.

Bukit Pondok; Penang.

O. PENANGENSIS, Stol. l.c. 1872, p. 265, pl. 10, fig. 7; Pfr. Mon. Pneumon. Suppl. III. 1876, p. 43; G. Nevill, Handl. 1878, p. 263; H. Crosse, Jour. Conch. XXVII. 1879, p. 338.

Bukit Pondok; Penang.

O. JAVANUS, Pfr. Malak. Bl. VII. 1860, p. 215, pl. 3, figs. 8-10; Mon. Pneumon. Suppl. II. 1865, p. 37.

Nungnang, Java.

O. SUMATRANUS, von Mart. Monatsber. Berl. Ak. 25 Feb. 1864; Pfr. Mon. Pneumon. Suppl. II. 1865, p. 37.

Sumatra.

(!) O. SPINIFERUS (CYCLOSTOMA), Morelet, = *Cyclostoma spiniferum*, Morelet, Jour. Conch. IX. 1861, p. 177 = *Opisthoporus spiniferus*, von Mart. Ostas. Zool. II. p. 113; Pfr. Mon. Pneumon. Suppl. III. p. 41.

Borneo.

O. PERTUSUS (CYCLOSTOMA), Morelet; Issel, Moll. Born. p. 75; Pfr. Mon. Pneumon. Suppl. III. p. 43 = *Cyclostoma pertusum*, Morelet, Jour. Conch. IX. 1861, p. 177.

Borneo.

23. PTEROCYCLOS, Benson.

Jour. Roy. As. Soc. I. 1832 and V. 1836; Zoological Journ. V. No. 20, p. 462.

Shell sub-discoid, largely umbilicate; aperture circular, the external layer overlapping the inner and dilated posteriorly with a distinct groove at the suture; operculum thick, composed of several spiral calcareous layers externally concave and horny within.

A small genus characteristic of the Indian region.

PTEROCYCLOS ALBERSI, Pfr. Zeitschr. f. Malak. 1847, p. 151; Chemn. 2nd edit. Cyclostoma, p. 197, pl. 28, figs. 1-5; Pfr. Mon. Pneumon. p. 45.

Perak; Kinta Valley (!), Selama (!).

PT. BREVIS (LITUUS), Martyn, = *Lituus brevis*, Martyn, Fig. of non-described shells, pl. 28c; Ed. Chenu (Bibl. Conch. II.) p. 21, pl. 8, fig. 2 = *Turbo petiverianus*, Wood, Suppl. pl. 6. fig. 2 = *Cyclostoma petiverianum*, Gray in Wood's Suppl. p. 36 = *Cyclostoma breve*, Pfr. in Chemn. 2nd edit. No. 180, p. 166, pl. 24, figs. 1-2 = *Myxostoma petiverianum*, Trosch. in Zeitschr. f. Malak. 1847, p. 44 = *Pterocyclos brevis*, Pfr. Zeitschr. f. Malak. 1851, p. 9; Consp. No. 46; Mon. Pneumon. p. 42.

India; Pulo Condor.

PT. PLANORBULUS, Lamarck, = *Cornu venatorium*, Chemn. Cab. IX. p. 104, pl. 127, figs. 1132-33 (?) = *Cyclostoma planorbula*, Lamarck, Encyclop. Méth. pl. 461, fig. 3 = *Cyclotus planorbulus*, Swains. Malacol. p. 336 = *Pterocyclos planorbulus*, Pfr. Consp. No. 47; Mon. Pneumon. p. 43.

Java (?); Borneo (?).

PT. TENUILABIATUS, Metc.; Pfr. Mon. Pneumon. p. 45 = *Cyclostoma tenuilabiatum*, Metc. Proc. Zool. Soc. 1851.

Borneo.

PT. BLANDI, Benson, Ann. and Magaz. VIII. 1851, Aug. pl. 5, fig. 1; Pfr. Mon. Pneumon. p. 49.

Pulo Susson.

PT. (?) SPIRACELLUM, A. Ad. and Reeve; Pfr. Mon. Pneumon. p. 50 = *Cyclostoma spiracellum*, A. Ad. and Reeve, Voy. Samar. Moll. p. 56, pl. 14, fig. 1; Pfr. Mon. Pneumon. p. 50.

Borneo.

PT. LABUANENSIS, Pfr. Proc. Zool. Soc. 1863; Mon. Pneumon. Suppl. II. p. 41.

Labuan.

PT. LOWIANUS, Pfr. Proc. Zool. Soc. 1863; Mon. Pneumon. Suppl. II. p. 41.

Labuan.

PT. SUMATRANUS, von Mart. Monatsber. Berl. Ak. 25 Feb. 1864; Pfr. Mon. Pneumon. Suppl. II. p. 42.

Sumatra.

PT. BATCHIANENSIS, Reeve, Conch. Icon. sp. 6, pl. 2; Pfr. Mon. Pneumon. Suppl. II. p. 43.

Batchian.

PT. (?) EUDAEDALEUS, Crosse, Jour. Conch. XVII. 1869, p. 187; Pfr. Mon. Pneumon. Suppl. III. p. 51.

Borneo.

24. SPIRACULUM, Pearson, 1833, Jour. R. As. Soc. II. p. 391; H. and A. Adams, Genera, p. 278.

Shell depressed, sub-discoid, with a thick periostraca, which is sometimes covered with small hairs; aperture circular; at the last whorl a sutural tube formed by the union of the outer layer of the shell over the channel on the penultimate whorl. By most authors this is regarded as a sub-genus of *Pterocyclos*.

SPIRACULUM (?) REGELSPERGERI, de Morgan, Le Naturaliste, VII. 1885, No. 9, p. 69 (*Cyclophorus*); O. von Möllendorff, Jour. As. Soc. Beng. LV. 1886, p. 308.

The last-named author says (l.c.) that the species is decidedly not a *Cyclophorus* but a *Pterocyclos*, which might be related to

Pt. albersi, Pfr., on account of the curious canaliculated suture. He adds: "De Morgan's mention of a tube, and of the fine membranaceous lamellæ of the operculum to render its fitting more hermetic, suggest a *Spiraculum* or *Rhiostoma* ;* but against the inclusion in the latter genus, it may be mentioned that the last whorl is not free."

Environs of Lahat and Pappan ; Kinta Valley ; Larut.

I collected three specimens, one on the road between Lahat and Goping, one at the mouth of the Diepang River, and one at Pappan, all in Perak.

S. KINTANUM, De Morgan, l.c. 1885, p. 69 = *Cyclophorus kintanum*, De Morgan, l.c. = *Spiraculum kintanum*, O. v. Möll. Jour. As. Soc. Beng. LV. p. 308.

Kinta Valley.

25. CYCLOPHORUS, Montfort, Conch. Syst. II. p. 290.

Shell globose, turbinate or depressed and discoid, well umbilicated ; peristome entire, thick, double, and reflected ; periostraca thick ; operculum horny, orbicular, thin, multispiral.

A large genus, which formerly included nearly 200 species, but has now been sub-divided into several genera. Even after this Pfeiffer enumerated about 250 species. They are principally tropical and Indian, but some of the species are particularly characteristic of the Malayan region.

CYCLOPHORUS CONFLUENS, Pfr. Proc. Zool. Soc. 1860, p. 140 ; Reeve, Conch. Icon. sp. 69, pl. 15 ; Pfr. Mon. Pneumon. Suppl. II. p. 60.

Borneo.

---

*It should be noted that in Chenu's "Manuel de Conchyliologie" the genus is always written *Registoma*, possibly Van Hasselt's genus, the etymology of which is ῥηγή and στόμα, but the derivation of *Rhiostoma* is from ἔιον, a promontory.

C. BANKANUS, von Mart. Ostas. Zool. II. p. 135; Pfr. Mon. Pneumon. Suppl. III. p. 101.

Banka Island.

C. MALAYANUS, Benson, — *Cyclostoma malayanum*, Bens. Ann. and Mag. Nat. Hist. 2nd series, X. p. 269 = *Cyclostoma volvulus* (*trochiformæ*, Lamarck), Souley. Voy. Bonite, Moll. pl. 30, figs. 18-21 = *Cyclotus* (?) *trochiformis*, M. E. Gray, Fig. Moll. Anim. pl. 303, fig. 11 (ex Souley.) *Cyclophorus malayanus*, Pfr. Malak. Bl. 1854, p. 82; Mon. Pneumon. Suppl. I. p. 42.

Malayan Peninsula.

C. DEBEAUXI, Crosse, Jour. Conch. XII, 1864, p. 42; Pfr. Mon. Pneumon. Suppl. II. p. 62.

Singapore.

C. TUBA, Sow. = *Cyclostoma tuba*, Sow. Proc. Zool. Soc. 1843, p. 83; Chemn. 2nd edit. Cycl. No. 183, p. 169, pl. 23, figs. 10-11; Souley. Voy. Bonite, Moll. pl. 30, figs. 25-27 = *Cyclophorus tuba*, Pfr. Zeitschr. f. Malak. 1847, p. 107; Consp. No. 68; Mon. Pneumon. p. 57; Gray, Catal. Cycloph. p. 16, No. 3.

Mount Ophir, Malacca.

C. PFEIFFERI, Reeve, Conch. Icon. sp. 11, pl. 3; Pfr. Mon. Pneumon. Suppl. II p. 64.

Pulo-Penang.

C. BORNEENSIS, Metc. *Cyclostoma borneense*, Metc. Proc. Zool. Soc. 1851; Chemn. 2nd edit. Cycloph. No. 384, pl. 47, figs. 1-3 = *Cyclophorus borneensis*, Pfr. Mon. Pneumon. p. 63.

Borneo.

C. PERDIX, Brod. and Sow. = *Cyclostoma perdix*, Brod. and Sow. Zool. Jour. V. p. 50 *Cyclostoma variegatum*, Val. Mus. Paris = *Cyclostoma aglae*, Sow. test. Mouss. Jav. Moll. p. 54 = *Cyclophorus perdix*, Pfr. Zeitschr. f. Malak. 1847, p. 107; Mon. Pneumon. p. 63.

Java.

C. ZOLLINGERI, Mouss. = *Cyclostoma zollingeri*, Mouss. Jav. Moll. p. 55, pl. 7, fig. 2 = *Cyclophorus zollingeri*, Pfr. Mon. Pneumon. p. 64.

Java.

C. CANTORI, Bens. = *Cyclostoma cantori*, Bens. Ann. and Mag. Nat. Hist. 2nd ser. VIII. p. 168; Chemn. new edit. p. 383, pl. 50, figs. 4-8 = *Cyclophorus cantori*, Pfr. Mon. Pneumon. p. 65; Mon. Pneumon. Suppl. I. p. 49; Gray, Cat. Phan. p. 44; H. and A. Adams, Genera II. p. 279.

Penang.

C. EXIMIUS, Mouss. *Cyclostoma eximium*, Mouss. Jav. Moll. p. 53, pl. 7, fig. 1; Chemn. 2nd edit. No. 227, pl. 33, figs. 1-2 = *Cyclophorus eximius*, Pfr. Mon. Pneumon. p. 69.

Java.

C. BELULUS, von Mart. Monatsber. Berl. Ak. 16 Jan. 1865, p. 52; Issel, Moll. Born. p. 69; Pfr. Mon. Pneumon. Suppl. III. p. 106.

West Borneo.

C. OCULUS CAPRI, Wood, = *Helix oculus capri*, Wood, Ind. pl. 32, fig. 7 = *Cyclostoma oculus capri*, Gray, Mus. Brit.; Reeve, Conch. Syst. pl. 184, fig. 11; Sow. Thes. No. 73, p. 115, pl. 25, fig. 96; Chemn. 2nd edit. No. 18, p. 26, pl. 3, figs. 5-6; Mouss. Jav. Moll. p. 52, pl. 6, fig. 2 = *Cyclostoma rafflesii*, Brod. and Sow. Zool. Journ. V. p. 50 = *Cyclostoma indicum*, Phil. Abbild. I. 5, p. 103, pl. 1, fig. 2 = *Cyclophorus oculus capri*, Gray, Catal. Cycloph. p. 20, No 23; Pfr. Mon. Pneumon. p. 87.

Java; Sumatra.

C. SEMISULCATUS, Sow. *Cyclostoma semisulcatum*, Sow. Proc. Zool. Soc. 1843, p. 62; Chemn. 2nd edit. No. 81, p. 86, pl. 11, figs. 1-2 = *Cyclophorus semisulcatus*, Gray, Catal. Cycloph. p. 20, No. 24; Pfr. Mon. Pneumon. p. 88.

Malacca.

C. CHARPENTIERI, Mouss. = *Cyclostoma charpentieri*, Mouss. Jav. Moll. p. 56, pl. 6, fig. 3; Mörch, Catal. Conch. p. 8 (*sharpentieri*), pl. 1, fig. 6 = *Cyclostoma incolumis*, var.? Chemn. 2nd edit. p. 30, pl. 8, figs. 10-12 = *Cyclophorus sharpentieri*, Pfr. Mon. Pneumon. p 89.

Java.

C. TAENIATUS, Pfr. = *Cyclostoma taeniatum* (*Cyclophorus*), Pfr. Proc. Zool. Soc. 1854, p. 301 = *Cyclophorus taeniatus*, Pfr. Mon. Pneumon. Suppl. I. p. 59.

Sumatra.

C. TENEBRICOSUS, Adams and Reeve, = *Cyclostoma tenebricosum*, Ad. and Reeve, Voy. Samarang, Moll. p. 57, pl. 14, fig. 6 = *Leptopoma tenebricosum*, Pfr. Consp. No. 171 ; Mon. Pneumon. p. 117 = *Cyclophorus tenebricosus*, Ad. Genera, p. 280 ; Pfr. Mon. Pneumon. Suppl. I. p. 76, II. p. 69.

Borneo.

C. BELLUS, von Mart. Malak. Bl. XX. 1872, p. 159 ; Pfr. Novit. Conch. IV. p. 126, No. 830, pl. 128, fig. 10 ; Mon. Pneumon. Suppl. III. p. 113.

Celebes.

C. METCALFEI, Issel, Moll. Born. 1874, p. 69, pl. 6, figs. 4-6 ; Pfr. Mon. Pneumon. Suppl. III. p. 113.

Sarawak, Borneo.

C. TROCHOIDES (LAGOCHEILUS), Stol. = *Lagocheilus trochoides* Stol. Journ. As. Soc. XLI. 1872, p. 273, pl. 10, fig. 15 ; = *Cyclophorus trochoides*, Pfr. Mon. Pneumon. Suppl. III. p. 123.

Penang.

C. STRIOLATUS (LAGOCHEILUS) Stol. = *Lagocheilus striolatus*, Stol. Jour. As. Soc. Beng. XLI. 1872, p. 271, pl. 10, fig. 16 = *Cyclophorus striolatus*, Pfr. Mon. Pneumon. Suppl. III. p. 123.

Penang.

C. REGELSPERGERI, De Morgan, Le Nat. VII. 1885, No. 9, p. 69 = *Spiraculum regelspergeri*, von Möllendorff, Jour. As. Soc. Beng. LV. 1886, p. 308.

Environs of Lahat and Pappan, the Valley of the Kinta River, Perak.

C. KINTANUM, De Morgan, l.c. 1885, p. 69 = *Spiraculum kintanum*, von Möllendorff, l.c.

Kinta Valley, Perak.

C. EXPANSUS, Pfr. (?) var. von Möllendorff, l.c. p. 309 ; G. Nevill, Handl. 1878, p. 269.
Bukit Pondok.

C. LOWI, de Morgan, l.c. 1885, p. 69 ; von Möllendorff, l.c. p. 309.
Kinta Valley ; Patani.

C. (LAGOCHILUS ?) TOWNSENDI, Crosse, Jour. Conch. XXVII. 1879, pp. 200, 339, pl. 8, f. 3 = *Lagocheilus*, n.sp. G. Nevill, Handl. 1878, p. 282 = *Cyclophorus baylei*, De Morgan, l.c. 1885, p. 69   *Lagochilus townsendi*, von Möllendorff, l.c. p. 309.

26. LEPTOPOMA, Pfeiffer, Zeitschr. f. Malak. 1847, p. 47.

A *Cyclophorus* with a thin operculum.

LEPTOPOMA ASPIRANS, Benson, von Möllendorff, l.c. p. 309.
Bukit Pondok.

27. ALYCÆUS, Gray, Proc. Zool. Soc. 1850.

Shell conical or depressed, very deep sutures, last whorl much swollen, constricted and twisted near the opening, which is round ; peristome double, the outer plate reflected ; operculum thin, circular, calcareous, with numerous whorls.

ALYCÆUS GIBBOSULUS, Stol. Jour. As. Soc. Beng. XLI. 1872, p. 268, pl. 10, fig. 14 ; Pfr. Mon. Pneumon. Suppl. III. p. 58.
Penang.

A. PERAKENSIS, Crosse, Jour. Conch. XXVII. 1879, pp. 206, 339, pl. 12. fig. 7 ; von Möllendorff, Jour. As. Soc. Beng. LV. 1886.
Bukit Pondok.
Crosse compares this with *A. jagori*, Mart., from Java. It is, however, well distinguished from this latter by its large size, bright yellow colour, the smaller number of its whorls, and its spiral sculpture (von Möllendorff).

A. DIPLOCHILUS, von Möllendorff, l.c. p. 310.
Bukit Pondok.

A. OLIGOPLEURIS, von Möll. l.c. p. 310.
Bukit Pondok.

A. MICRODISCUS, von Möll. l.c. p. 311.
The peculiar distortion of the last whorl, which first descends after the constriction, and is again deflected towards the aperture, separates this minute species from all forms known (von Möllendorff).
Bukit Pondok.

A. PARVULUS, von Möll. l.c.
Another minute form, still smaller than the last to which it appears somewhat related. It differs, however, in the constriction being nearer the aperture, almost regular last whorl, the broad outer and very prominent inner peristome (von Möll.).
Bukit Pondok.

A. MICROCONUS, von Möll. l.c.
By the conical shape, the regular last whorl and the reticulate sculpture this small species is very well distinguished from all Indian *Alycæi*.
Bukit Pondok.

A. JOUSSEAUMEI, De Morgan, Le Nat. VII. 1885, No. 9, p. 70; von Möll. l.c. p. 312.
Limestone hills of the valley of the Kinta, summit of Mt. Lano.

A. CHAPERI, De Morgan, l.c. p. 70, probably = *A. gibbosulus*, Stol. *Ita* von Möll.
Penang; Bukit Pondok.

Family DIPLOMMATINACEÆ, Benson.

(Including the genera *Paxillus*, *Palaina*, *Arinia* and *Diplommatina*).

28. DIPLOMMATINA, Benson, Ann. and Mag. Nat. Hist. 1849, Sept. p. 193.

Shell sub-oval, with the slightest trace of an umbilical slit; peristome interrupted expanded; operculum thin, between testaceous and horny, with a projecting thin claw.

Shells belonging to the Indian region amounting to about 30 species, but some of uncertain position, which extend to New Zealand, Lord Howe's Island and Australia. The family may be said to be represented partly in southern Asia and its islands.

Animal with long and filiform tentacles, with sessile eyes on the posterior base; foot short. The name of the genus refers to two lobes on each tentacle at the base behind, on each of which there is an eye. The species abound in masses of decayed vegetable matter, or under stones in damp situations, and beneath trees on the shady sides of mountains. I found a good many on a dead tree which had been felled in the clearing of a coffee plantation. At daybreak in the morning I generally found one or two walking about. This was probably *D. mirabilis*. The genus *Paxillus* is founded on a smooth reversed species from Borneo.

DIPLOMMATINA CONCINNA, H. Adams, Proc. Zool. Soc. 1872, p. 13, pl. 3, fig. 22; Issel, Moll. Born. p. 77; Pfr. Mon. Pneumon. Suppl. III. p. 74.

Borneo.

D. CANALICULATA, von Möll. Jour. As. Soc. Beng. LV. 1886, p. 312.

Bukit Pondok.

D. NEVILLI, Crosse, Jour. Conch. XXVII. 1879. pp. 203, 339, pl. 8, fig. 2 (*Palaina*); von Möll. l.c. p. 313.

Bukit Pondok.

D. CROSSEANA, Godwin-Aust. and G. Nev. Proc. Zool. Soc. 1879, p. 738, pl. 60, figs. 3, 3a.

Bukit Pondok.

D. MIRABILIS, Godwin-Aust. and G. Nev. l.c. p. 739, pl. 60, figs. 4a, 4b; von Möll. l.c. p. 313.

Bukit Pondok.

D. SUPERBA, Godwin-Aust. and G. Nev. l.c. p. 739, pl. 60, figs. 5, 5a (*Palaina*).

Bukit Pondok.

29. OPISTHOSTOMA, Crosse and Nevill, Jour. de Conch. XXVII. 1879, pp. 197, 205, 339.

Shell with the upper whorls obliquely deflected ; last whorl constricted, thin, inflated, finally sinistrally ascending close to the upper whorls ; aperture reversed, almost vertical, rounded ; peristome continuous and duplicated ; operculum normal. Habitat the same as the last genus. Scarcely a dozen species.

OPISTHOSTOMA PAULUCCIE, Crosse and Nevill, Jour. de Conch. XXVII, 1879, pp. 197, 205, 339, pl. 8, fig. 1 ; Godwin-Aust. and G. Nev. Proc. Zool. Soc. 1879, p. 738, pl. 9, figs. 2, 2a, 2b ; von Möll. Jour. As. Soc. Beng. LV. 1886, p. 313.

Bukit Pondok.

O. PERAKENSE, Godwin-Aust. and G. Nev. l.c. p. 738, pl. 60, figs. 1, 1a, 1b ; von Möll. l.c. p. 313.

Bukit Pondok.

O. CRESPIGNYI (PLECTOSTOMA). H. Adams (Coll. 1.) = *Plectostoma De Crespignii*, H. Adams, Ann. and Mag. Nat. Hist. 3rd ser. XV. p. 177 (Pfr. Mon Hel. V. p. 437) = *Opisthostoma decrepignyi*, Paetel, Catal. p. 119 = *O. crespignyi*, Pfr, Mon. Pneumon. Suppl. III. p. 68.

Labuan, Borneo.

Family PUPININÆ, Pfr.

30. PUPINA, Vignard, Ann. Sc. Nat. Vol. XVIII. 1829, p. 440.

Shell sub-cylindric like *Pupa*, thin, transparent, smooth, very shining ; mouth not quite round ; the columella margin with a deep notch anteriorly and a tooth posteriorly ; peristome simple : operculum in all the family orbicular, thin, horny, with numerous gradually increasing whorls from a central nucleus.

PUPINA ARTATA, Bens. ; von Möll. Jour. As. Soc. Beng. LV. 1886, p. 311.

Perak.

P. ARULA, Bens.; von Möll. l.c.
Bukit Pondok.

P. AUREOLA, Stol. Jour. As. Soc. Beng. XLI. 1872, p. 267, pl. 10, figs. 11-12; Pfr. Mon. Pneumon. Suppl. III. p. 148.
Penang.

P. PFEIFFERI, H. Adams, Proc. Zool. Soc. 1865, p. 416, pl, 21, figs. 11-12 = *P. pfeifferiana*, H. Adams, Proc. Zool. Soc. 1869, p. 275 = *P. pfeifferi*, Pfr. Mon. Pneumon. Suppl. III. p. 149.
Island of Batchian.

P. JUNGHUHNI (RHEGISTOMA), Herklots — *Rhegistoma janghuhni*, Herk. Mus. Lugdun = *Pupina junghuhni*, Pfr. Mon. Pneumon. Suppl. III.p. 151.
Java.

P. AMBOINENSIS (CALLIA), von Mart. — *Callia amboinensis*, von Mart. Monatsber. Berl. Ak. 16 Jan. 1865, p. 53 — *Pupina amboinensis*, Pfr. Mon. Pneumon. Suppl. III. p. 154.
Amboyna.

P. VESCOI, Morelet, Rev. et Mag. Zool. 1862, p. 479; Crosse and Fisch. Jour. Conch. XI. p. 372; Pfr. Mon. Pneumon. Suppl. II. p. 94.
Pulo Condor.

P. SUPERBA, Pfr. Proc. Zool. Soc. 1855, p. 118; Mon. Pneumon. Suppl. I. p. 94.
Sumatra.

31. MEGALOMASTOMA, Guilding; Swainson, Malacology, pp. 186 and 336.

Shell cylindrical resembling *Pupa*, but has a horny operculum; spire not thickened; teeth or fold on the pillar none.

MEGALOMASTOMA ANOSTOMA, Bens. Pfr. Malak. Bl. 1854, p. 89 = *M. sectilabrum*, Pfr. Mon. Pneumon. p. 133; Chemn. new edit.

p. 377, pl. 47, figs. 11-12; Gray, Cat. Phan. p. 93 = *M anostoma*, Pfr. Mon. Pneumon. Suppl. I. p. 85.

Labuan, Borneo.

M. LEFERI, Morelet = *Cyclostoma leferi*, Morelet, Jour. Conch. IX. 1861, p. 176 = *Megalomastoma leferi*, von Mart. Ostas. Zool. II. p. 154; Pfr. Mon. Pneumon. Suppl. III. p. 138.

Borneo.

M. DORIAE, Issel, Moll. Born. 1874, pl. 67, pl. 6, figs. 18-19; Pfr. Mon. Pneumon. Suppl. III. p. 138.

Sarawak, Borneo.

M. (COPTOCHILUS) SECTILABRUM, Gould; von Möll. Jour. As. Soc. Beng. LV. 1886, p. 314.

Perak; Larut; Penang.

32. HYBOCYSTIS, Benson, 1859, Annals and Mag. Nat. Hist. 3rd ser. IV. p. 90.

This remarkable and exceedingly interesting genus, which forms one of the peculiar features of the terrestrial molluscan fauna of the Malay Peninsula, deserves the fullest details in this list. Fortunately its history as a species has been well marked out by M. P. Fischer in the "Journal de Conchyliologie"(XXV. 3rd series, 1885, p. 180), an epitome of whose researches will now be given.

The genus was proposed by Benson in 1859 for a Burmese shell which had been hitherto described as a species of *Megalomastoma*, and in its young stages as a species of *Otopoma*. Some years before Dr. Gould, the American naturalist, had described the same shell, for which he had proposed the generic name of *Pollicaria*; but as the genus was insufficiently defined, and included species of different genera, Benson's genus has been preferred as complying with every condition of necessary exactness.

The shell is ovoid and pupiform, but deviating from its axis in the last whorls in the manner of certain species of *Streptaxis*. The ante-penultimate whorl is much developed and flattened in front above the mouth, which is sub-circular and angular anteriorly in young specimens, which also present a little canaliculate prolongation, which is obliterated little by little as the animal is developed, leaving when completely closed only the appearance of a triangular area traversed longitudinally by a linear scar, and leaving in that state a rounded double peristome. Internal lip relatively less thick, deeper coloured, and more shining; external reflected, but not always perfectly united with the inner. Operculum testaceous, somewhat thick, with a central nucleus, and composed of two plates; external face multispiral, slightly concave in the middle; internal face few whorls, also slightly concave in the middle; margin with a feeble keel.

The foot is not divided as in the Cyclostomidæ, where there are two longitudinal parts independent of each other for crawling. The animal is long, with a very thin mantle, whose anterior border is simple and not papillose; head and muzzle short, thick, the latter grooved transversely on its upper face; buccal orifice, when open, oval, and showing the extremity of the radula, but when the mouth is closed it is a simple slit; tentacles short, thick, transversely striate, slightly constricted at the base, of a uniform reddish color; eyes at the external base well pigmented and placed on short, obtuse, and slightly convex peduncles; foot thick, fleshy, wide, short, oval, obtuse, truncate in front, round behind. There is a large pedal sinus in front, but no trace of that longitudinal division which is common in the family of Cyclostomidæ, but the foot is rather that of the family of Cyclophoridæ. The upper part of the foot carries the operculum, the adherence of which is circular, with an umbilicated non-central projection, which corresponds to the nucleus of the internal face, so that half the organ is free, like the genus *Cyclophorus*. The sexes are distinct, the females being a little larger in size. The mouth has two mandibular plates, brown, chitinous, and solid, visible to the naked eye, but when magnified displaying a facetted structure roughly hexagonal or rounded. This may possibly be some arrangement connected with the eyes of the animal, or a facetted eye-structure like that which exists in the head of insects. All the Cyclophoridæ have similar organs. The radula has the following formula $(2, 1, 1, 2) \times 66$. It is long, a little curved at the end, but relatively shorter than amongst the most of the Cyclophoridæ. The teeth are in oblique rows from the median line to the outer margin. The central teeth are a little oblong, slightly constricted in the centre like an hour-glass, and widely and roundly notched at the base. There is a central wide, short, obtuse cusp, with the rudiment of a lateral one. The first lateral teeth are larger, oblique, elongate, with a narrow base, curving over outwardly on the summit in a direction opposite to the other teeth. The free edge is bicuspid, the outer short, wide, obtuse, the inner small and short. The two marginal teeth are bicuspid, the internal cusp more feeble than the external, which is triangular.

M. Fischer, in the "Manuel de Conchyliologie," p. 71, gives his reasons for classing *Hybocystis* between *Pupina* and *Cataulus*, but he admits that it differs from the majority of Cyclophoridæ by its bicuspid marginal and lateral teeth, and the obtuse cusps of the median tooth. These characters united to those of the shell and of the operculum determine the genus. In the position of *Hybocystis* Dr. Pfeiffer takes a different view, and places it in the great family of Cyclostomaceæ, in the sub-family Cyclotea. Stoliczka (Jour. As. Soc. Beng. 1871, p. 150) agrees with M. Fischer.

The following is the explanation of the figures given in the plate :—

Fig. 1. Animal of *Hybocystis elephas*, De Morgan, from a female specimen preserved in alcohol. The head and foot are shown in front—M, edge of mantle ; T, tentacles ; E, eye ; F, sole of foot.

Fig. 2. Male specimen of the same ; head and foot shown in front—M, mantle ; T, tentacles ; E, eye ; F, foot ; V, verge.

Fig. 3. Same male specimen shown in profile from the right side—T, tentacle ; B, buccal orifice ; F, foot ; V, verge.

Fig. 4. Radula of do.—A, central tooth ; B, lateral tooth ; C, first marginal tooth ; D, second marginal tooth.

Fig. 5A. Portion of one of the mandibular plates (very much enlarged).

Fig. 5B. Details of do., on a much larger scale.

Figures 1, 2, 3 are magnified two diameters.

HYBOCYSTIS ELEPHAS, De Morgan, Le Nat. VII. 1885, No. 9, p. 70 ; von Möll. Jour. As. Soc. Beng. LV. 1886, p. 314.

Perak.

H. JOUSSEAUMEI, De Morgan, l.c. p. 70 ; von Möll. l.c. p. 315.

Valley of the Plus river.

Family HYDROCENIDÆ.

33. GEORISSA, Blanford, 1864.

Ann. and Mag. Nat. Hist. 3rd series, XIII. 1864, p. 463 ; ibid. 4th series, III. 1869, p. 173.

Type *Hydrocena pyxis*, Benson.

Shell resembling that of *Hydrocena*, imperforated, small, conical, amber or reddish-coloured, spirally sulcated or striated.

Animal furnished with hemispherical lobes in the place of tentacles ; eyes normal ; foot short, rotund. Operculum semi-oval, no spiral structure as in Helicina ; excentrically striated, testaceous, transparent.

GEORISSA MONTEROSATIANA, Godwin-Austen and G. Nevill, Proc. Zool. Soc. 1879, p. 739, pl. 59, fig. 6 ; von Möll. Jour. As. Soc. Beng. LV. 1886, p. 316.

Bukit Pondok.

G. SEMISCULPTA, Godwin-Austen and G. Nevill, l.c. p. 740, pl. 59, fig. 3, 3a ; von Möll. l.c. p. 316.

Bukit Pondok.

FRESHWATER MOLLUSCA.

Sub-order OPISOPHTHALMA.

Family TRUNCATELLIDÆ.

These animals have a distinct bi-lobed muzzle with flat sub-triangular tentacles, and a sub-spiral horny operculum.

1. TRUNCATELLA, Risso, Hist. Nat. de l'Europe, IV. p. 121.

Shell solid, cylindrical in its young state, truncated in the adult; whorls rounded; mouth oval; peristome complete, reflected; operculum horny, thin, with a lateral nucleus.

Animal furnished with a retractile bifid muzzle proboscis-shaped. There are about 15 species, tropical or sub-tropical, found in salt and fresh water.

TRUNCATELLA VALIDA, Pfr. Mon. Auric. p. 184; Zeitschr. f. Malak. 1846, p 182, No. 1; Kust. Mon. p. 11, No. 7, pl. 2, figs. 7, 8, 19, 21, 23.

Philippines, Baclayon, Capul, New Caledonia, and Malay Peninsula.

TR. MARGINATA, Küst. Mon. p. 12, No. 8, pl. 2, figs. 24-26; Pfr. Mon. Auric. p. 186.

Labuan, Borneo; Malacca.

TR. AURANTIA, Gould, Exp. Sh. 1846, p. 39, Ed. 1851, pl. 8, fig. 125; Pfr. Mon. Pneumon. Suppl. I. p. 6.

Mangsi Island, Borneo.

TR. SCALAROIDES, von Mart. Monatsber. Berl. Ak. 25 Febr. 1864; Pfr. Mon. Pneumon. Suppl. II. p. 7.

Amboyna.

Family MELANACEÆ.

2. MELANIA, Lamarck, Hist. Nat. Animaux s. Vertèbres.

Shell more or less turreted, generally wrinkled or nodulous, mostly covered with a black or olive epidermis; spire elongated, generally more or less eroded towards the apex ; columella smooth, arched ; aperture ovate, entire, sometimes attenuately channelled at the base ; lip simple.

Animal: disk short and slight; head proboscis-shaped, subconical, truncated, with the tentacles distant and subulate, having the eyes on the outer side and sometimes at the base, sometimes more advanced ; mantle fringed ; operculum horny.

Univalve shells chiefly inhabiting the tropical rivers of India, the Indian Archipelago and tropical North America. About 160 species have been described, but these are capable of great reduction.

MELANIA FOEDA, Lea, Proc. Zool. Soc. Lond. 1850; Brot, Mater. III. p. 33, pl. 3, tig. 4; Brot, Melanidæ, Conchylien Cabinet I. p. 51.

Java.

M. ANGULIFERA, Brot, Mater. III. p. 32, pl. 2, fig. 9 ; Melanidæ, Conch. Cab. I. p. 51.

Java.

M. PARVA, Lea, — *Pachychilus parvum*, Lea, Proc. Ac. Nat. Sc. Philad. 1856 = *Melania crassilabrum*, Reeve, Conch. Icon. f. 221 = *Paludomus cyanostomus*, Morelet, Jour. Conch. 1864, p. 288 = *Melania parva*, Brot, Melan. (Conch. Cab. I.) p. 55.

Sarawak, Borneo ; Siam ; New Caledonia, (?)

M. SULCOSPIRA, Mouss. Jav. Moll, pl. 9, fig. 3 ; Brot, Melan. p. 56 = *Sulcospira typica*, Trösch. Gebiss der Schnecken.

Java.

M. PERFECTA, Mouss. Jav. Moll. pl. 22, fig. 5 ; Reeve, Conch. Icon. fig. 84 = *Melanoides perfecta*, H. and A. Ad. Gen.= *Melania perfecta*, Brot, Melan. p. 79.

Amboyna ; Maros, Celebes.

M. WALLACEI, Reeve, Conch. Icon. fig. 66 ; Brot, Melan. p. 80 — *M. constricta*, Mouss. MSS.

Celebes ; Macassar.

M. VARIABILIS, Benson, Jour. As. Soc. Calcutta, 1835 ; Hanley and Theobald, Conch. Ind. pl. 109, figs. 2-6 = *Melanatria variabilis*, Gray, Guide Syst. distrib.= *Melania herculea*, Reeve, Conch. Icon. fig. 4 a. b. = *Melanoides herculea*, H. and A. Ad. Gen. *Melania variabilis*, Brot, Melan. p. 85.

Java ; Burmah.

M. SUMATRENSIS, Brot, Melan. p. 87.

Sumatra, Java.

M. EPISCOPALIS, Lea, Proc. Zool. Soc. 1850 ; (?) Reeve, Conch. Icon. fig. 12 ; Brot, Melan. p. 97.

Malacca.

M. INFRACOSTATA, Mouss. Jav. Moll. p. 65, pl. 10, fig. 3 (not Reeve) ; Brot, Melan. p. 98 = *M. episcopalis*, Lea, var. Brot, Catal. of Rec. Mel. p. 280, No. 80.

Java.

M. BROOKEI, Reeve, Conch. Icon. fig. 207 = *M. episcopalis*, Lea, Catal. Rec. Melan.= *M. pontificalis*, v. d. Busch, Zeitschrift f. Malak. 1853, p. 178 = *M. brookei*, Brot, Melan. p. 99.

Borneo.

M. AGRESTIS, Reeve, Conch. Icon. f. 140 = *M. coarctata*, Lam. var. Brot, Mater. I. p. 42 = *M. agrestis*, Brot, Melan. p. 101.

Borneo.

M. CIRCUMSTRIATA, Metc. Proc. Zool. Soc. 1851, p. 73 ; Reeve, Conch. Icon. fig. 205 = *Melanoides circumstriata*, H. and A. Ad. Gen.= *Melania circumstriata*, Brot, Melan. p. 101.

Borneo.

M. clavaeformis, Brot, Melan. p. 103.
Borneo.

M. torquata, v. d. Busch, Phil. Abbildg. pl. 1, fig. 18 ; Mouss. Jav. Moll. pl. 12, fig. 2 ; Brot, Melan. p. 110 = *M. terebra*, Reeve, Conch. Icon. fig. 59 ; Hanley and Theobald, Conch. Ind. pl. 71, figs. 8-9.
Java ; Bengal.

M. soolooensis, Reeve, Conch. Icon. fig. 31 ; Brot, Melan. p. 105.
Sulu.

M. zollingeri, Brot, Mater. II. pl. 2, fig. 1, p. 42 ; Melan. p. 111.
Java.

M. crenulata, (Desh.) var. tirouri (Fér.); Desh. in Lam. An. s. V. No. 18 ; Chenu, Man. Conch. fig. 1986 ; H. and A. Adams, Gen.; Brot, Melan. p. 114.
Celebes.

M. crenulata (Desh.) var. porcata, Jonas, Zeitschr. f. Malak. 1844, p. 50; Phil. Abbildg. pl. 4, fig. 19 ; Mousson, Moll. Jav. pl. 11, fig. 4 ; Brot, Melan. p. 114.
Java.

M. semicancellata, v. d. Busch, Phil. Abbildg. pl. 3, fig. 2 ; Reeve, Conch. Icon. fig. 37*b;* Brot, Melan. p. 118 = *M. lævis*, (Gray) Reeve, Conch. Icon. fig. 40 (not Gray) = *M. phlebotomum*, Reeve, Conch. Icon. fig. 105.
Java.

M. obesula, Brot, Melan. p. 121.
Java.

M. aculeus, Lea, Trans. Amer. Phil. Soc. Philad. V. pl. 19, fig. 72 ; Hanley, Conch. Misc. fig. 33 = *M. latronum*, Tarnier, MSS. = *M. subulata*, Sow. Man. Conch. 313 = *M. aculeus*, Brot, Melan. p. 122.
Java.

M. UNIFORMIS, Q. and G. Voy. Astrol. pl. 56, figs. 30-35; Desh. in Lam. An. s. V. No. 26; H. and A. Ad. Gen.; Brot, Melan. p. 124 — *M. fulgida*, Reeve, Conch. Icon. fig. 24 = *M. baculus*, Reeve, Conch. Icon. fig. 130.

Menado, Celebes; Philippines.

M. ANTHRACINA, v. d. Busch, Phil. Abbildg. pl. 3, fig. 3; Brot, Melan. p. 127.

Java (?).

M. TEREBRIFORMIS, Brot, Mater. I. p. 51; Melan. p. 144 = *M. terebra*, v. d. Busch, Phil. Abbildg. pl. 1, fig. 17; Reeve, Conch., Icon. fig. 46.

Java.

M. TURRIS, Brot, Mater. III. p. 38, pl. 2, fig. 11; Melan. p. 146.

Borneo.

M. ACICULA, Brot, Mater. III. p. 39, pl. 3, figs. 8-9; Melan. p. 154.

Labuan, Borneo.

M. SEMIORNATA, Brot, Rev. Zool. 1860, pl. 16, fig. 5; Melan. p. 159.

Java.

M. ARCTE-CAVA, Mouss. Jour. Conch. 1857, p. 161; Brot, Melan. p. 165 = *M. arcticava*, Mouss. in Reeve, Conch. Icon. fig. 71.

Bajumatil, Java.

M. MOLUCCENSIS, Q. and G. Voy. Astrol. pl. 56, figs. 22-25; Desh. in Lam. An. s. V. No. 24; Brot, Mater. III. p. 44, pl. 3, fig. 3 (not Reeve, Conch. Icon.); Melan. p. 166 = *Juga moluccensis*, (Q. and G.) H. and A. Ad. Gen.

Amboyna; Halmaheira.

M. MONILE, Mouss. Jour. Conch. 1857, p. 162; Brot, Melan. p. 173.

Java (?); Moluccas.

M. ORNATA, v. d. Busch, Phil. Abbildg. pl. 1, figs. 15-16; Brot. Melan. p. 173.
Java.

M. TRISTIS, Reeve, Conch. Icon. fig. 121; Brot, Melan. p. 175.
Java.

M. FULGURANS, Hinds, Ann. Mag. N. H. XIV. p. 9; Reeve, Conch. Icon. fig. 55; Chenu, Man. Conch. fig. 1993; H. and A. Ad. Gen.; Brot, Melan. p. 183.
Moluccas: New Ireland; Formosa.

M. LABUANENSIS, Brot, Mater. III. p. 41; Melan. p. 184.
Labuan, Borneo.

M. PAPUENSIS, Q. and G. Voy. Astrol. pl. 56, figs. 45-47; Desh. in Lam. An. s. V. No. 27; Brot, Mater. III. p. 45; Melan. p. 186.
Moluccas (?).

M. DISTINGUENDA, Brot, Melan. p. 190 = *M. pyramus* (Bens.) Reeve, Conch. Icon. fig. 51 (not Bens. nor v. d. Busch).
Borneo.

M. AMABILIS, v. d. Busch, in Reeve, Conch Icon. fig. 223 = *M. pulchra*, v.d. Busch, Malak. Blät. 1858, p. 35 = *M. amabilis*, Brot, Melan. p. 192.
Celebes.

M. SUBSUTURALIS, Metc. Proc. Zool. Soc. 1851, p. 73; Brot, Melan. p. 197 = *M. metcalfei*, Reeve, Conch. Icon. fig. 212.
Borneo.

M. DISJUNCTA, Brot, Melan. p. 198.
Borneo.

M. INHONESTA, v. d. Busch, Phil. Abbildg. pl. 4, fig. 5; (?) Reeve, Conch. Icon. fig. 226; (?) Mousson, Jav. Moll. p. 71; Brot, Melan, p. 206 = *M. ovalana*, Mouss. Jour. Conch. 1870, p. 208.
Java; Ovalau.

M. CREPIDINATA, Reeve, Conch. Icon. fig. 120; Brot, Melan. p. 238.
Java; Borneo.

M. JAVANICA, v. d. Busch, MSS. (Philippi states that this is a MS. name of van den Busch) ; Brot, Catal. Rec. Mel. No. 200 ; Melan. p. 246 = *M. coarctata* (Lam.) Phil. Abbildg. pl. 4, fig. 20 ; Reeve, Conch Icon. fig. 22.

Java.

M. TUBERCULATA, Müll. Verm. Ter. No. 378 ; Chemn. IX. p. 189 ; Phil. Abbildg. pl. 1, fig. 19 ; Reeve, Conch. Icon. fig. 87 ;= *Melanoides tuberculata* (Müll.), H. and A. Ad. Gen.= *Melania fasciolata*, Lam. An. s. V. No. 16 *M. suturalis*, Phil. Abbildg. p. 4, fig. 17 = *M. tuberculata*, Brot, Melan. p. 247.

Siam ; Java ; Malta ; Madagascar ; India ; Ceylon, &c.

M. CYLINDRACEA, Mouss. Jav. Moll. pl. 11, fig. 9 ; Brot, Melan. p. 252 = *Melanoides cylindracea* (Mouss.), H. & A. Ad. Gen.

Java.

M. FONTINALIS, Phil. Abbildg. pl. 5, fig. 7 ; Brot, Melan. p. 253.

Pulo-Pinang.

M. MALAYANA, Issel, Moll. Born. p. 100 : Brot, Melan. p. 253 *M. tuberculata*, Müll. var. *malayana*, Issel, l.c.

Sarawak, Tangiou-Datou, Borneo.

M. PARREYSSII, Brot, Melan. p. 254.

Java (?).

M. UNIFASCIATA, Mouss. Jav. Moll. pl. 11, fig. 8 ; Brot, Melan. p. 262 = *Melanoides unifasciata* (Mouss.), H. and A. Ad. Gen.

Malang, Java.

M. SCABRA, Müll. in Hanl. Theob. Conch. Ind. pl. 73, figs. 1-4 ; Brot, Melan. p. 266 = *Buccinum scabrum*, Müll. Verm. p. 136, No. 329 = *Helix scabra*, Chemn. Conch. pl. 136, figs. 1259-60 *Melania spinulosa*, Lam. An. s. V. No. 12 ; Q. and G. Voy. Astrol. pl. 56, figs. 12-14 ; Mouss. Jav. Moll. pl. 11, figs. 11, 12 = *Plotia scabra* (Lam.), H. and A. Ad. Gen.; Chenu, Man. Conch. fig. 1943.

Java ; India ; Ceylon ; New Guinea, &c.

M. GRANUM, v. d. Busch, Phil. Abbildg. pl. 1, fig. 7; Mouss. Jav. Moll. pl. 12, fig. 3; Reeve, Conch. Icon. fig. 219; Brot, Melan. p. 270 = *M. scrabella* (Phil.), Mouss. Jav. Moll. pl. 12, fig. 2 = *Plotia granum* (v. d. B.), H. and A. Ad. Gen.

Java.

M. MYURUS, Brot, Rev. Zool. 1860, pl. 16, fig. 3; Melan. p. 271.

Java; Borneo (?).

M. ACANTHICA, Lea, Proc. Zool. Soc. 1850; Hanley, Conch. Misc. fig 8; Brot, Melan. p. 278 = *M. spinulosa* (Lam.) Reeve, Conch. Icon. fig. 156 a-b (not Lam.) = *Tiara acanthica* (Lea), H. and A. Ad. Gen.

Manila; Negros; Moluccas.

M. EUDICOSTIS, Mouss. Brot, Melan. p. 280.

Amboyna.

M. DIADEMA, Lea, Proc. Zool. Soc. 1850; Reeve, Conch. Icon. fig. 174; Brot, Melan. p. 293 = *Tiara diadema*, H. and A. Ad. Gen.

Philippines; Amboyna.

M. CYBELE, Gould, Proc. Bost. S.N.H. 1847; Mouss. Jour. Conch. 1865, p. 199, 1870, p. 214 = *Tiara cybele* (Gould), H. and A. Adams, Gen. = *T. crenularis* (Desh.) H. and A. Ad. op. c. = *Melania cybele*, Brot, Melan. p. 294.

Sumatra; Fijis; Philippines.

M. SETOSA, Swainson, Quart. Jour. Sci. 1824; Gray, Zool. Jour. I. pl. 8, figs. 6-8; Reeve, Conch. Icon. fig. 186; Brot, Melan. p. 297 = *Buccinum aculeatum*, Lister, Hist. s. syn. meth. Conch. pl. 1055, fig. 8 = *Helix amarula*, var. Chemn. IX. pl. 134, figs. 1220-21.

Amboyna.

M. ORIENTALIS, A. Adams (*Plotea*), Proc. Zool. Soc. 1853, p. 99; Reeve, Conch. Icon. fig. 181; Brot, Melan. p. 300 = *Tiara orientalis* (Ad.) H. and A. Ad. Gen. = *Melania hippocastanum*, Brot, Rev. Zool. 1860, pl. 16, fig. 1.

New Caledonia; Eastern Archipelago.

M. WINTERI, v. d. Busch, Phil. Abbildg. pl. 1, figs. 1-2 ; Mouss. Jav. Moll. pl. 12, fig. 1 ; Reeve, Conch. Icon. fig. 157 ; Brot, Melan. p. 301 = *Plotea winteri* (v. d. B.) H. and A. Ad. Gen. ; Chenu, Man. Conch. fig. 1945.

Java.

M. HERKLOTZI, Petit, Jour. Conch. 1853, pl. 7, fig. 10 ; Brot, Melan. p. 303 = *M. dura*, Reeve, Conch. Icon. fig. 187 = *M. strobilus*, Reeve, op. c. fig. 214 = *Plotea herklotzi* (Petit), H. and A. Ad. Gen.

Java.

M. RUDIS, Lea, Proc. Zool. Soc. 1850 ; Reeve, Conch. Icon. fig. 172 ; Brot, Melan. p. 305 ; Mater. II. pl. 1, fig 7 = *M. microstoma*, Lea, Proc. Zool. Soc. 1850 ; Hanl. Conch. Misc. fig. 58 = *Tarebia microstoma* (Lea), H. and A. Ad. Gen.

Batchian, Moluccas.

M. SEMICOSTATA, Phil. Abbildg. pl. 4, fig. 12 ; Brot, Melan. p. 308 = *Sermyla semicostata* (Phil.), H. and A. Ad. Gen. = *Melania riquetti* (Gratel.) Mouss. Jav. Moll. p. 76.

Samarang, Java.

M. ARMILLATA, Lea, Proc. Zool. Soc. 1850 ; Brot, Mater. II. pl. 1, fig. 12 ; Melan. p. 309 = *Tarebia armillata* (Lea), H. and A. Ad. Gen.

Java (?) ; India.

M. CELEBENSIS, Q. and G. Voy. Astrol. pl. 56, figs. 26-29 ; Desh. in Lam. An. s. V. No. 25 ; Brot, Mater. II. pl. 1, fig 13 ; = *Tarebia celebensis* (Q. and G.) H. and A. Ad. Gen. ; Chenu, Man. Conch. fig. 2014 = *Vibex celebensis* (Q. and G.) Gray, Guide Syst. Dist. = *Melania celebensis*, Brot, Melan. p. 317.

Menado, Celebes ; Arrow Island.

M. CRENIFERA, Lea, Proc. Zool. Soc. 1850 ; Reeve, Conch. Icon. fig. 169 ; Brot, Melan. p. 323 = *Tarebia crenifera* (Lea), H. and A. Ad. Gen.

Java.

M. GRANOSPIRA, Mouss. Jour. Conch. 1857, p. 161 ; Brot, Mater. II. pl. 1, fig. 10 ; Melan. p. 324.

Bali.

M. COFFEA, Phil. Abbildg. pl. 2, fig. 4 ; Brot, Melan. p 326 = *Tarebia coffea*, (Phil.) H. and A. Ad. Gen.

Java (?).

M. ASPERULA, Brot, Mater. II. pl. 1, fig. 11 ; Melan. p. 327 = *M. semigranosa* (v. d. B.) Mouss. Jav. Moll. p. 74.

Java.

M. LIRATA, Benson, Glean. of Sc. 1830, II. ; Jour. As. Soc. Beng. 1836, V. 782 ; Reeve, Conch. Icon. fig. 170 = *M. lineata* (Gray), Hanl. Theob. Conch. Ind. pl. 71, fig. 7 ; Phil. Abbildg. pl. 3, fig. 7 ; Mouss. Jav. Moll. pl. 10, fig. 6 — *M. semigranosa*, v. d. Busch, Phil. Abbildg. pl. 1, fig. 13 ; Reeve, Conch. Icon. fig. 1, 67 = *M. flavida*, Mouss. Jav. Moll. pl. 10, fig. 5 — *Tarebia lineata*, H. and A. Ad. Gen.= *T. flavida* (Dunker), H. and A. Ad. Gen.= *Melania lirata*, Brot, Melan. p. 329.

Java ; Bengal, &c.

M. RIQUETTII, Gratel. Mém. plus. esp. Moll. pl. 3, fig 28 ; (?) Hanl. and Theob. Conch. Ind. pl. 71, fig. 10 ; Brot, Melan. p. 333 = *M. harpula*, Dunker, Phil. Abbildg. pl. 3, fig. 6 — *Tarebia riquettii* (Gratel.), H. and A. Ad. Gen. Rec. Moll. *Sermyla harpula* (Dkr.), H. and A. Ad. op. cit.

Philippines ; Java (?).

3. CLAVIGER, Haldemann, Silliman's Journal, 1842.

Shell turreted, solid, with a series of longitudinal keels or nodules ; aperture attenuated at the base, sub-canaliculate ; right margin sinuous towards the base, produced in an arcuate manner, furnished with three short and deep parallel plates : operculum few-whorled, sinistral, with a sub-marginal basal nucleus.

CLAVIGER HIPPOCASTANUM, Reeve. Conch. Icon. fig. 188 ; Brot, Melan. p. 360.

Borneo.

4. FAUNUS, Montfort, Conch. Syst. II. p. 427.

Shell subulate, with an attenuated spire, whorls numerous, smooth, covered with a blackish periostraca ; mouth notched in front, columella lip rather thick, with posterior callosity ; outer lip spreading with a posterior sinus. (Chenu, who figures the common species here described, only admits it as a sub-genus of *Pirena*). A tropical form with half a dozen species at most, belonging to tropical Asia, the Philippines, and Western Polynesia.

FAUNUS CANTORI, Reeve, Conch. Icon. fig. 2 ; Brot, Melan. p. 414 = *Pirena cantori*, Reeve, Conch. Icon. fig 2, China.

Penang.

F. ATER, L. = *Strombus ater*, L. Syst. Nat. XII. p. 1213; Chenu. pl. 135, fig. 1227   *Nerita atra*, Müll. Verm. No. 375 = *Cerithium fluviatile*, Féruss. Syst. Conch. p. 69 = *Pirena atra* (L.) Mouss. Jav. Moll. pl. 10, fig. 1 ; Reeve, Conch. Icon. fig. 5 = *Faunus ater* (L.) H. and A. Ad. Gen. ; Gray, Guide Syst. Dist. ; Chenu, Man. Conch. fig. 2080 ; Brot, Melan. p. 410 = *Pirena terebralis*, Lam. An. s. V. No. 1 ; Q. and G. Voy. Astrol. pl. 56 -- *Pirena picta*, Reeve, Conch. Icon. fig. 3 (stat. juv.)

Moluccas ; New Guinea ; New Ireland ; Java ; Ceylon ; Amboyna, &c.

5. PHILOPOTAMIS, Layard, Ann. and Magaz. Nat. Hist. 1855, p. 138.

Operculum with the apex superior, paucispiral ; nucleus *subbasal*, dextral.

PHILOPOTAMIS OLIVACEUS, Reeve, Conch. Icon. fig. 5 ; Brot, Gatt. Palud. p. 16.

6. PALUDOMUS, Swainson, Treatise on Malacology, p. 340.

Shell thick, sub-globose or conical, solid, imperforate, smooth or tubercular, covered with an olivaceous epidermis ; spire shorter than the aperture, often eroded ; aperture ovate ; inner lip convex, thickened ; outer lip acute, the margin slightly reflexed ; operculum annular, nucleus sub-central.

Animal with the mantle margin fringed. Most of the species from India and Ceylon.

PALUDOMUS ISSELI, Brot, Gatt. Palud. p. 31 = *P. crassus*, (v. d. B.), Issel, Moll. Born. p. 95.

Sarawak, Borneo.

P. BROTI, Issel, Moll. Born. p. 92 ; Brot, Gatt. Palud. p. 32.

Sarawak, Borneo.

P. LUTEUS, H. Adams, Proc. Zool. Soc. 1874, p. 585 ; Brot, Gatt. Palud. p. 46 = *P. moreleti*, Issel, Moll. Born. p. 93.

Sarawak, Borneo.

Note.— The Bivalves are reserved for another paper.

EXPLANATION OF PLATES.

PLATES XXVII-XXX.

Fig. 1.— *Hybocystis elephas*. Animal (♀). See p. 1073.
Fig. 2.— ,, ,, ,, (♂). See p. 1074.
Fig. 3.— ,, ,, ,, Profile view.
Fig. 4.— ,, ,, Radula. See p. 1075.
Fig. 5a.— ,, ,, Portion of one of the mandibular plates, very much enlarged.
Fig. 5b.— ,, ,, The same, much more highly magnified.
(The above drawings are those of M. Fischer from the " Journal de Conchyliologie, XXV., 1885, p. 179.)

Figs. 6-7.—Shell of *Bulimus perversus*, L.
Figs. 8-9.—Shell of *Hybocystis elephas*, De Morgan.
Figs. 10-11.—Operculum of ,, ,, ,,
Fig. 12.—*Bulimus* sp. (?) (Borneo)
Fig. 13.—*Cyclophorus* sp. Thaiping, Perak.
Fig. 14.—*Helix algira*, L.
Fig. 15.—*Alycaeus gibbus*, Férussac.
Fig. 16.—*Pirena terebralis*, Lamarck.
Fig. 17.—*Helix citrina*, L.
Fig. 18.—*Cyclophorus* sp. Pulo-Pankore, Perak.
Fig. 19.— *Melania episcopalis*, Lea.
Fig. 20.—*Nanina brookei*, Adams & Reeve.
Fig. 21.— ,, *sumatrensis*, Mousson.
Fig. 22.— ,, *mendaiensis*, Semper.
Fig. 23.— ,, *hugonis*, Pfeiffer.

BIBLIOGRAPHY OF MALAYAN LAND AND FRESHWATER SHELLS.

Adams, H. and A. The Genera of Recent Mollusca arranged acccording to their Organization. 2 vols. and 1 vol. plates. London, 1858.

Adanson, M. Histoire Naturelle du Sénégal. Paris, 1757.

Albers, J. Chr. Die Heliceen nach natürlicher Verwandtschaft systematisch geordnet. Leipsic, 1860.

Annals and Magazine of Natural History. London, 3 series. 2 vols. annually.

Austen, H. H. Godwin. Land and Freshwater Mollusca of India, 1882.

——— and G. Nevill. Shells from Perak and the Nicobar Islands. Proc. Zool. Soc. Lond. 1879, pp. 734-740 (9 sp.).

Beck, H. Index Molluscorum praesentis aevi Musei Principis Christiani Frederici. Hanover, 1837 (two parts only were published).

Benson, W. H. Gleanings of Science.

——— In Ann. and Magaz. Natural History. IX. 1842.

——— In Jour. Asiatic Society of Bengal, V. 1836, and VII. 1838.

Blainville, D. de. Dictionnaire des Sciences Naturelles, XXXII. 1824. Art. Mollusques.

Blanford, W. T. and H. F. Contributions to Indian Malacology, 12 parts. Calcutta, 1860 to 1870 (10 plates).

Born, I. von. Testacea Musei Caes. Vindobon. dispos. et descr. Vindob. 1780. (Vienna).

Brot, A. Catalogue of Recent Species of the Family Melanidæ. New York, 1868.

——— Die Gattung Paludomus. Nürnberg, 1861.

——— Die Melaniaceen (Melanidæ) in Abbildungen nach der Natur mit Beschreibungen. Nürnberg, 1874. Conchylien Cabinet von Martini und Chemnitz.

Bruguière, J. G. Encyclopédie Méthodique. Vers. 2 vols. Paris, 1789-92.

Canefri, C. Tapparone. Zoologia del viaggio intorno al globo della regia fregata Magenta durante gli anni, 1865-1868. Malacologia, 1874 (Jour. Conch. 1874, p. 319).

Chemnitz. Systemat. Conchylien-Cabinet. (Begun at Nuremberg in 1784, extending over some years. A second edition also published).

Chenu, J. C. Manuel de Conchyliologie et de Paléontologie Conchyliologique. 2 vols. Paris, 1859.

Conchyliologie, Journal de. Paris, I. 1851, and thenceforth a volume in every succeeding year.

Crosse, H. Mollusques nouveaux de Perak. Jour. de Conch. XXVII. 1879, pp. 198-208 (5 sp.).

———— Faune malacologique de Perak. Ibid. pp. 336-340 (18 sp.).

Delessert, B. Recueil de Coquilles décrites par Lamarck et non encore figurées. Paris, 1841.

Dillwyn, L. W. A descriptive Catalogue of Recent Shells. 4 vols. London, 1817.

Dohrn, H. In Malakozoologische Blätter. Cassel, 1854-1877.

Draparnaud, J. P. F. Tableau des Mollusques terrestres et fluviatiles de la France. Paris, 1801.

———— Histoire Naturelle des Mollusques terrestres et fluviatiles de la France. Paris, 1805.

Ehrenberg, C. G. Symbolæ Physicæ. Moll. 1831.

Férussac, D'A. Histoire Naturelle Générale et Particulière des Mollusques Terrestres et Fluviatiles, 1819-21. Paris, 2 vols. with atlas of plates.

Freycinet, L. de. Voyage autour du monde, 1824.

Gaimard (Quoy et). Voyage de l'Astrolabe, Zoologie, 1832.

Gmelin, J. F. Systema Naturæ Linnæani (13th ed.), I. 1790.

Godwin-Austen H. H. Land and Freshwater Mollusca of India. Calcutta, 1882.

———— (and G. Nevill). Shells from Perak and the Nicobar Islands. Proc. Zool. Soc. 1879, pp. 734-740 (9 sp.).

Gould, A. A. Boston Society of Natural History.
———— United States Exploring Expedition during the years 1838-42, under the command of Ch. Wilkes. XII. Mollusca and Shells. Boston, 1852.
Grateloup. Actes de la Société Linnéene de Bordeaux, 1841.
———— Mémoires sur plusieurs espèces de coquilles nouvelles ou peu connues de Mollusques (Lin. Soc.) Bordeaux, 1841.
Gray, M. E. Figures of molluscous animals selected from various authors. London, 1850.
———— J. E. Nomenclature of Molluscous Animals and Shells in the collection of the British Museum. Pt. 1, Cyclophoridæ, 1850.
———— Catalogue of Pulmonata or air-breathing Mollusca in the collection of the British Museum. Pt. 1, Phaneropneumona, 1852.
———— Guide to the Systematic Distribution of Mollusca in the British Museum, London, 1857.
———— In Annals of Philosophy. (New series). IX. 1825.
———— Spicilegia Zoologica, 1830.
———— New edition of Turton's Manual, 1840.
———— Synopsis of the Contents of the British Museum, 1840.
———— Ed. 44a., 1842.
———— In Annals of Natural History, VI. 1840.
———— In Loudon's Magazine, I. (New series).
Guérin-Méneville, F. E. Revue et Magasin de Zoologie pure et appliquée. 2nd series, IX. 1857 ; XIX. 1867.
Guilding, S. L. Conchological Papers. See Swainson, "Shells and Shell-fish," pp. 182-336.
Günther, A. Zoologischer Jahresbericht. Leipsic, 1861.
Hanley. Conchological Miscellany. London, 1858.
———— and Theobald. Conchologia Indica. London, 1876.
Hasselt, Van. Allgemeine Konst-en Letterbode.
Herklots, J. A. Fauna Molluscorum et Vermium Hollandiæ. Haarlem, 1862.
Hinds, R. B. Zoology of the Voyage of H.M.S. "Sulphur." Mollusca. Pt. III. 1845.

Hochstetter, F. von. Reise der Oesterreichischen Fregatte "Novara." 2 vols. 4to. Vienna, 1864.
Hombron, (et Jacquinot). Voyage au Pôle Sud. Zoologie V. Livr. 24, pl. 11-12.
Humphrey. Museum Calonianum Catalogue. London, 1797.
Hutton, T. In Jour. As Soc. Bengal, III. 1834, VIII. 1838.
Issel, A. Molluschi Borneense. Genova, 1874.
Jacquinot (Hombron et). Voyage au Pôle Sud.
Kämmerer, C. L. Die Conchylien im Cabinette des H. Erbprinzen von Schwarzburg. Rudolstadt, 1786.
Knorr, G. W. Vergnügen der Augen und des Gemüths. I. 1757, II. 1764, VI. 1773.
Küster, H. C. In Chemnitz Conchylien-Cabinet. Neue Ausg.
Lamarck. Histoire Naturelle des Animaux sans Vertèbres. Two editions, the second by Deshayes. 8 vols. Paris, 1838.
Lea, J. Observations on the genus *Unio*, &c. I. 1832, III. 1842.
———— Transactions of the American Philosophical Society of Philadelphia, VII. New series, 1841.
———— Proceedings of the Academy of Natural Science. Philadelphia.
———— New Unionidae, Melanidae, &c., chiefly of the United States. (3 parts). Philadelphia, 1866-69.
Le Guillou. Revue Zoologique par la Société Cuviérienne, 1838-1847.
Lesson, R. P. Voyage de la Coquille. Paris, 1830.
Linnaeus. Systema Naturae. 13 editions. Turton's English Translation from Gmelin's posthumous edition in seven volumes. London, 1806.
Lister, M. Historia s. synopsis meth. Conchyliorum ad viv. delin. 4 parts. London, 1685.
Malakozoologische Blätter (Menke und Pfeiffer). Cassel, 1854-78.
Martens, E. von. Monatsber. Berlin. Akademie.
———— Die preussische Expedition nach Ost-Asien. Zoologischer Theil.
Martyn, T. Figures of non-described shells, 1789.

Menke, C. Th. Synopsis Methodica Molluscorum. 1st edit., 1828, 2nd edit., 1830.

———— (und Pfeiffer). Malakazoologische Blätter. Cassel, 1854-1878.

Metcalfe, W. Proceedings of the Zoological Society, 1851.

Möllendorff, O. F. von. Journal of the Asiatic Society of Bengal, LV. 1886. "On the Land Shells of Perak."

Montfort. Histoire naturelle, générale et particulière des Mollusques. Faisante suite au Buffon de Sonnini, 1799-1805.

Mörch, O. A. L. Catalogus conchyliorum, quæ reliquit C. P. Kierulf, 1852.

Morelet, A. Testacea novissima insulæ Cubanæ et Americæ Centralis, 1849. Pt. 2, 1851.

Morgan, J. de. Note sur quelques espèces nouvelles de Mollusques terrestres, recueillis dans la Péninsule Malaise. Le Naturaliste VII. 1885, pp. 68-70.

Mousson, A. Die Land- und Süssw. Moll. von Java. Zurich, 1849.

Müller, O. F. Vermium terrestrium et fluviatilum Historia. Hanover, I. 1773, II. 1774.

Natural History, Annals and Magazine of. London, 3 series. 2 vols. annually.

Nevill, G. Hand-list of the Mollusca in the Indian Museum. Calcutta, 1878.

———— (Godwin-Austen and). Shells from Perak and the Nicobar Islands. Proc. Zool. Soc. 1879, pp. 734-740.

Paetel, Fr. Molluscorum systema et catalogus. Malak. Blätt. 1869, p. 204.

———— Catalog der Conchylien-Sammlung; nebst Uebersicht des angewandten Systems, 1873.

Pfeiffer, L. Monographia Heliceorum Viventium. Leipsic, 1868. 8 vols.

———— Nomenclator Heliceorum Viventium. Opus Postumum. Cassellis, 1881.

———— Novitates conchologicæ. II. 1860-66, III. 1866-67.

———— Symbolae ad Historiam Heliceorum. Cassel, 1841.

Pfeiffer, L. Versuch einer Anordnung der Heliceen nach natürlichen Grüppen, in Malakoz. Bl. II. 1855.

———— Monographia Pneumonopomorum Viventium. Cassel, 1852.

———— Conspectus Cyclostomaceorum emendatus et auctus. 1852.

Philippi, R. A. Abbildungen und Beschreibungen neuer oder wenig gekannter Conchylien. Bd. I. 1842-45, II. 1845-47, III H. 1, 1847.

Quarterly Journal of Science. London.

Quoy et Gaimard. Voyage de l'Astrolabe, 1832.

Reeve, L. Conchologia Iconica. 20 vols. London (the publication extending over a long series of years).

Revue et Magasin de Zoologie pure et appliquee. Paris, 1857-67.

Risso, A. Histoire Naturelle des principales productions de l'Europe méridionale, et particulièrement de celles des environs de Nice et des Alpes maritimes. IV. 1826.

Rossmässler, E. A. Iconographie der Land- und Süsswasser-Mollusken. 12 vols. published between 1835 and 1844.

Scopoli. Introductio ad historiam naturalem. Prague, 1777.

———— Deliciæ Floræ et Faunæ Insubricæ, 1786. [Prague (?)].

Semper, C. Reisen im Archipel de Philippinen. Wiesbaden, 1877.

Shuttleworth, R. J. Diagnosen neuer Mollusken. Nos. 1-3, 1852. Also papers in the Mittheilungen der Naturforsch. Gesellschaft in Bern, 1852 and 1843.

Souleyet, Voyage autour du monde (1836-37) sur la corvette La Bonite, par MM. Eydoux et Souleyet. 2 vols., and atlas. Paris, 1841.

Sowerby, G. Thesaurus Conchyliorum. London, 1855.

———— Conchological Manual. London, 1839.

Stoliczka, F. Journal of the Asiatic Society of Bengal, XLII. 1873, p. 16.

Swainson, W. M. Zoological Illustrations, London, 1820-21, II. 2nd series, 1831-32.

———— In Brand's Journal, Apr. 1828.

Swainson, W. M. A Treatise on Malacology or Shells and Shellfish. London, 1840.
Tapparone-Canefri, C. Zoologia del viaggio intorno al globo della regia fregata Magenta durante gli anni, 1865-1868. Malacologia, 1874 (Jour. Conch. 1874, p. 319).
Theobald (and Hanley). Conchologia Indica. London, 1876.
Troschel, F. H. Das Gebiss der Schnecken, zur Begründung einer natürl. Classification untersucht. Lief. I. 1856, II. 1857.
Tryon, Geo. W. Structural and Systematic Conchology. Philadelphia. Vol. I. of the Pulmonata, 1885. Work not yet completed.
Valenciennes. Archives du Muséum. Paris.
Van Hasselt. Allgemeine Konst-en Letterbode.
Vignard. Ann. Sc. Nat. XVIII. 1829.
Wood, W. Index tetaceologicus. (London, 1825, 2nd edit., with supp.) Edit. Sylv. Hanley, 1856.
Zeitschrift für Malakozoologie und Malakozoologische Blätter. Menke und Pfeiffer. Vollständig v. Beginn. an. 1844-76. 34 Bde. Hann. und Cassel. 8 m. Kpfrt.
Zelebor, J. Systemat. Verzeichniss der im Erzherzogthum Oesterreich bisher entdeckten und Land- Süsswässer-Mollusken, Wien, 1851.
Zollinger in Peterm. geog. Mittheil. (V. p. 464).
Zoological Society (of London), Proceedings of.

NOTES AND EXHIBITS.

Mr. Ogilby exhibited a specimen of a deep-sea fish (*Chlorophthalmus nigripinnis*), originally described by Dr. Günther in the Ann. of Nat. Hist., 1878, and figured in Vol. XXII. of the "Challenger Reports." The original specimens were taken by the "Challenger" naturalists off Twofold Bay, in 120 fathoms; the specimen exhibited to-night, was captured, a few days ago, off Port Jackson in 70 fathoms, the only other occasion on which the species has been met with since its discovery.

Mr. Ogilby also exhibited a photograph of *Acanthias Blainvillii*, not hitherto recorded from New South Wales, and one of a variety of *Acanthoclinus littoreus*, originally described by Forster in Cook's Voyage, the former having been taken in deep water off Port Jackson, the latter under stones between tide marks at Lord Howe Island.

Mr. Brazier exhibited a spherical stone about $\frac{1}{2}$ inch in diameter, found in the crop of a Goura pigeon (*G. Albertisi*, Salvad.), from Hall Sound, New Guinea. Also a tube of fresh-water shells (*Segmentina australiensis*, E. A. Smith) from Waterloo Swamps.

Mr. MacDonnell showed under the microscope an interesting exhibit of Rotifers (*Megalotrocha* sp.), living in clusters on pond weed.

Mr. Burnell exhibited two living Slow-worms (*Typhlops nigrescens*) from Wentworthville near Parramatta.

Mr. Deane exhibited a remarkable excrescence on a root of *Monotoca elliptica*, found by Mr. J. F. Fitzhardinge in the neighbourhood of Sydney; a specimen of an apodal lizard (*Delma impar*) found by Mr. C. F. Price of Arable, near Cooma, where the species is said to be abundant in basaltic country; and examples of nodular masses enclosing fossils, occurring abundantly in a slaty rock in a cutting near Bredbo on the Goulburn to Cooma Railway.

WEDNESDAY, 29TH AUGUST, 1888.

The President, Professor Stephens, M.A., F.G.S., in the Chair.

The following gentlemen were introduced as visitors—Mr. J. Dennant, F.G.S., Mr. G. Sweet, and Mr. F. G. A. Barnard of Victoria; Mr. J. C. Ross, B.Sc., F.G.S. of Bathurst, and Mr. C. A. Smith, F.C.S. of Sydney; Mr. R. L. Jack, F.G.S., Queensland.

MEMBERS ELECTED.

Messrs. H. S. Rohu, Sydney, and Mr. Bourne, Anatomical Museum, Sydney University, were elected Members of the Society.

The President announced :—

(1) That the Council had elected Mr. W. M. Bale, F.R.M.S., of Melbourne, a Corresponding Member of the Society.

(2) That two Excursions had been arranged for the ensuing month :—

    (a) September 15th—To Waterfall. Members to meet at Redfern Railway Station to proceed by the 8·22 a.m. train.

    (b) September 29th—To the Nepean River. Members to meet at Penrith Railway Station on the arrival of the 9 a.m. train from Sydney.

DONATIONS.

"Illustrated Catalogue of the Museum of Comparative Zoology at Harvard College. No. VII.—Revision of the Echini." By Alexander Agassiz. Five Pamphlets on Entomological Subjects, by Herr J. Faust. *From the Hon. W. Macleay, F.L.S., &c.*

Catalogue synonymique et systématique des Coléoptères de la Tribu des Carabides." Par J. B. Géhin ; "Catalogus Coleopterorum Lucanoidum." Auctore, Major F. J. Sidney Parry, F.L.S., 3rd Edition. *From T. G. Sloane, Esq.*

"Journal of the Royal Microscopical Society, London, 1888." Part 3. *From the Society.*

"The Journal of the Bombay Natural History Society." Vol. III., No. 2 (1888). *From the Society.*

"Mémoires de la Société de Physique et d'Histoire Naturelle de Genève." Tome XXIX. Seconde Partie (1886-87). *From the Society.*

"Mémoires de la Société Zoologique de France, pour l'Année 1888." Vol. 1, Nos. 1-3 ; "Bulletin." Tome XIII., Nos. 4 and 5 (1888). *From the Society.*

"Proceedings of the Zoological Society of London, for the year 1888." Part I. ; "Abstract of Proceedings, 19th June, 1888." *From the Society.*

"Feuille des Jeunes Naturalistes." No. 213 (July, 1888). *From the Editor.*

"Bulletin de la Société Belge de Microscopie." XIV. Année No. 7 (1888). *From the Society.*

"Records of the Geological Survey of India." Vol. XXI. Part 2 (1888). *From the Director.*

"L'Académie Royale de Copenhague – Bulletin pour 1887." No. 3 ; "Bulletin pour 1888." No. 1. *From the Academy.*

"Zoologischer Anzeiger." XI. Jahrg. Nos. 282 and 283 (1888). *From the Editor.*

"Proceedings of the Asiatic Society of Bengal." Nos. II. and III. (1888); "Journal," n.s. Vol. LVI., Part ii., No. 4 (1887); Vol. LVII., Part ii., No. 1 (1888). *From the Society.*

Monatliche Mittheilungen des Naturwissenschaftl. Vereins des Reg.-Bez. Frankfurt." Jahrg. V., Nos. 9-12 (Dec., 1887—March, 1888); "Societatum Litterae, 1887." No. 12 (Dec.); "1888." Nos. 1-4 (Jan.—April). *From the Society.*

"Iconography of Australian Species of ACACIA and Cognate Genera." Decades IX.-XI. By Baron Ferd. von Mueller, K.C.M.G., M. and Ph.D., F.R.S. *From the Premier of Victoria through the Librarian, Public Library, Melbourne.*

"Catalogue of Books added to the Radcliffe Library, Oxford University Museum, during the year 1887;" "List of Donations (1887.") *From the Library.*

"The Victorian Naturalist." Vol. V., No. 4 (August, 1888). *From the Field Naturalists' Club of Victoria.*

"Report of the Committee of Management of the Technological, Industrial, and Sanitary Museum of New South Wales for 1887." *From the Curator.*

Transactions and Proceedings and Report of the Royal Society of South Australia." Vol. X. (1886-87). *From the Society.*

"Mémoires et Publications de la Société des Sciences, des Arts et des Lettres du Hainaut." IVe. Série. Tomes IX. et X. (1887-1888). *From the Society.*

"Catalogue of the Minerals and Rocks in the Collection of the Australian Museum;" "Catalogue of Mammalia in the Collection of the Australian Museum." By G. Krefft, F.L.S., &c. (1873). *From Edward R. Deas Thomson, Esq.*

"Bulletin of the American Geographical Society." Vol. XX., No. 2 (1888). *From the Society.*

"The Journal of Comparative Medicine and Surgery." Vol. IX., No. 3 (1888). *From the Editor.*

"Bulletin of the Museum of Comparative Zoology at Harvard College, Cambridge, U.S.A." Vol. XIII., No. 9 (1888). *From the Curator.*

"The Australasian Journal of Pharmacy." Vol. III., No. 32 (August, 1888). *From the Editor.*

"The American Naturalist." Vol. XXII. No. 257 (May 1888). *From the Editors.*

"Société Royale Malacologique de Belgique—Procès-Verbal." (July-Dec., 1887). *From the Society.*

"Australian Museum, Sydney—Report of the Trustees for 1887." "Catalogue of Fishes—Part I. Recent Palæichthyan Fishes." By J. D. Ogilby, F.L.S. *From the Trustees.*

P.L.S.N.S.W. (2nd Ser.) Vol. 3   PL. 27

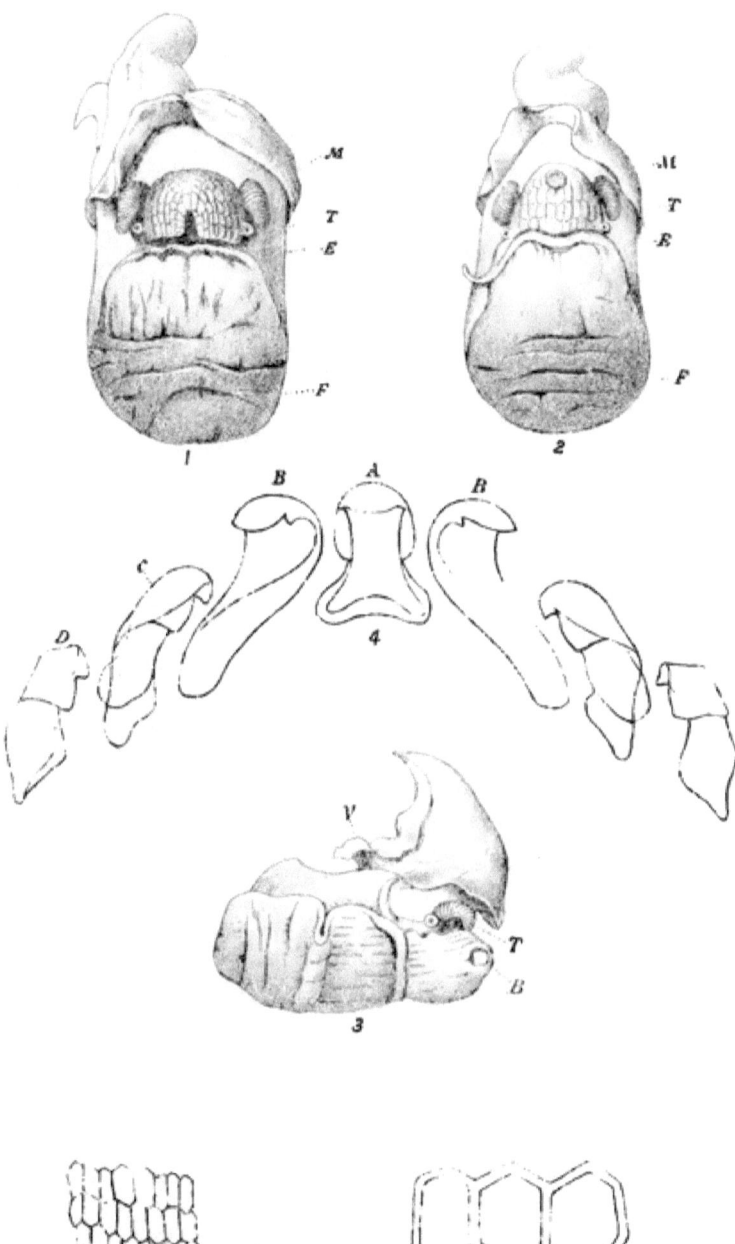

S. Sedgfield lith.

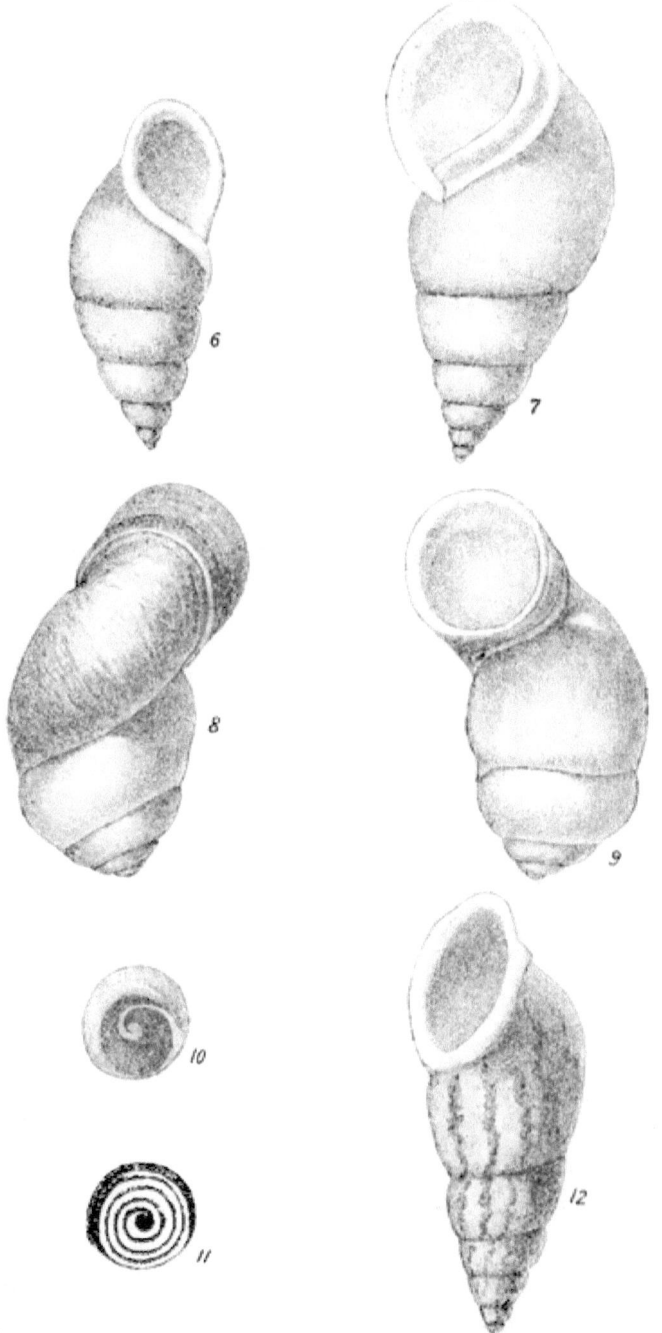

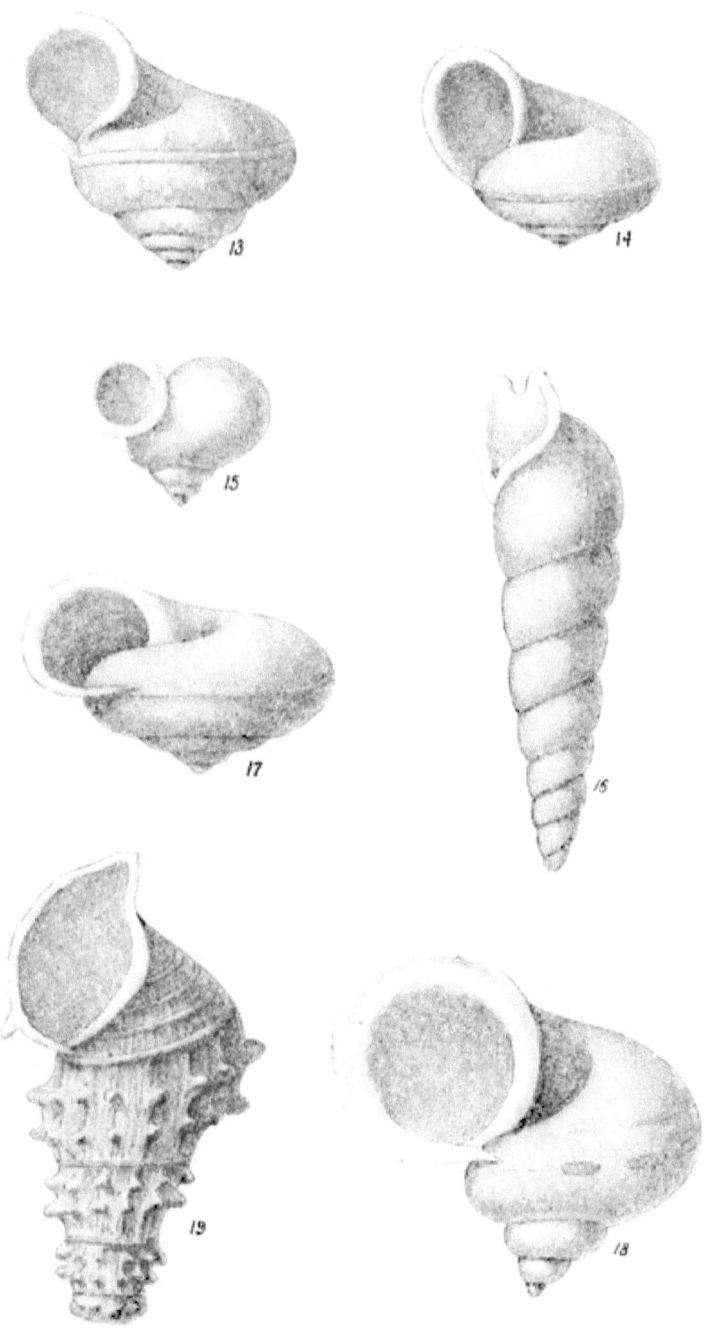

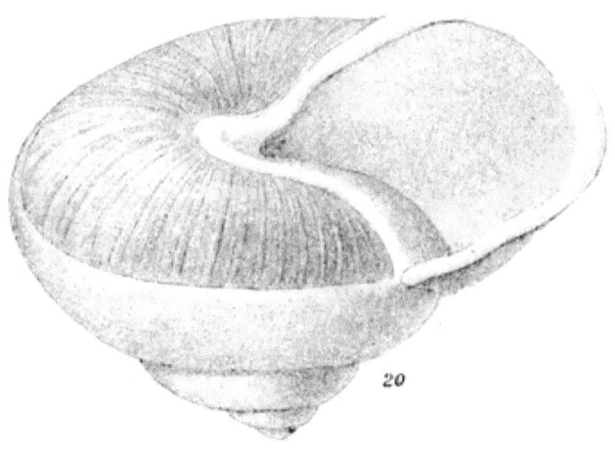
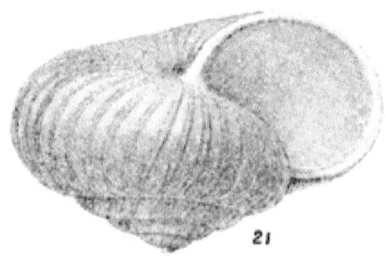

www.ingramcontent.com/pod-product-compliance
Lightning Source LLC
Chambersburg PA
CBHW020150170426
43199CB00010B/976